LIFE AFTER 50

LIFE AFTER 50
THE ROAD TO LONGEVITY

Dr. Paul M. Valliant

MILL CITY PRESS

Copyright © 2012 by Dr. Paul M. Valliant.

MILL CITY PRESS

Mill City Press, Inc.
212 3rd Avenue North, Suite 290
Minneapolis, MN 55401
612.455.2294
www.millcitypublishing.com

All rights reserved. No part of this publication may be reproduced, stored in a retrieval system, or transmitted, in any form or by any means, electronic, mechanical, photocopying, recording, or otherwise, without the prior written permission of the author.

ISBN-13: 978-1-938223-50-1
LCCN: 2012946593

Cover Design by Alan Pranke
Typeset by Kristeen Ott

Printed in the United States of America

To my mother Marion, whose daily activities exemplify her quest for longevity.

CONTENTS

Acknowledgments ix

PREFACE xi
Fountain of Youth

CHAPTER ONE 1
The Human Journey

CHAPTER TWO 25
Physiological Aging

CHAPTER THREE 55
Successful Aging

CHAPTER FOUR 71
Physical Health
Exercise:
Diet:

CHAPTER FIVE 89
Stress and Midlife Crises

CHAPTER SIX 99
Human Sexuality

CHAPTER SEVEN 113
Finances and Lifestyle

CHAPTER EIGHT 127
Housing and Retirement

CHAPTER NINE 141
Aging Alone or with Others

CHAPTER TEN 147
Final Passage

EPILOGUE 161
Nanotechnology a New Millennium

References 167

APPENDIX 187
Natural Foods and Alternative Health

Index 219

ACKNOWLEDGMENTS

When I turned 50, my search for longevity expanded. Many friends of similar age commented on the physiological and emotional changes they experienced after age 50. It wasn't clear whether these effects were caused by chronological or psychological factors. Research on this topic led me to believe that aging was not some disease but a stage of life. I began to see a course of travel which one should focus on their journey toward longevity. Interviews with seniors and information gathered from researchers and journalists have provided some scope to this book; to them I extend my gratitude. Last, Stan Koren deserves special thanks for his evaluation and commentary.

PREFACE

THE FOUNTAIN OF YOUTH

Rule #1: Seniors must live each day to the fullest.

Life after 50, the Road to Longevity was written to provide seniors with an understanding of the best ways of coping with aging. Many baby boomers will be in good physical, emotional and mental health at 50, while others will be tempered by the storms of aging. While some will be ready to retire after age 50, others will be motivated to work because of their interesting professions. And others will be forced to continue working because of their economic needs. By the time the reader completes this book, he or she will have better insight regarding ways of making aging a better journey.

During the past two decades, there has been a transition to a health conscious society. Much of this can be attributed to the lifestyle changes adopted by people searching to increase their longevity. The new age of healthful living has inspired many to re-evaluate their lives. Exercise, diet and lifestyle have become the new panacea paving the way for those who seek the fountain of youth.

Approximately 500 years ago, Ponce de Leon travelled from Spain to the New World in his search for longevity. This Spanish explorer believed the Island of Bimini, off the east coast of Florida, had enriched waters known for their restorative powers to cure Ponce's age related disorders. Some historians posit that his travels to Bimini did not provide him with his dream of longevity and thus he continued his search for the "fountain of youth" in nearby Florida. What one can surmise from this popular piece of history is that Ponce de Leon and countless others were in actuality searching for a lifestyle which could slow aging. Today, seniors undertake the annual winter ritual to Florida to escape the ravages of winter.

From the research which I have evaluated over the past three decades, it would seem there is no actual elixir which can restore one's body, but only a series of events to assist in slowing the aging process. Life After 50 the Road to Longevity, will make reference to a host of factors including genetics, diet, exercise, stress reduction, and cognitive enrichment which can assist seniors in their journey.

Genetics is one of the most important factors. Some people are born with sound genetics by virtue of their inherited DNA. At the basis of their gene pool are long strand telomeres which allow the cells to divide without undergoing deterioration. Unlike people with short strand telomeres, those with long strand telomeres don't age as quickly. Telomerase an enzyme must be available in the cell, to arrest the telomeres from breaking down after the cell has divided. Research has shown that a diet which includes astragalus can make the enzyme telomerase readily available to the cell.

Daily exercise also strengthens the telomeres, cells and organ systems thus slowing the aging process. Research indicates that people who exercise regularly, age more slowly than those who do not engage in physical activity. Some studies have found that on average, those who involve themselves in regular exercise at least 4 times a week have the physical ability of people who are ten years younger.

Diet is also an important factor. Those who eat food products which are less processed and most similar to a natural state product (ie. vegetables, fruit) are at an advantage because natural food products have abundant vitamins and antioxidants which remove waste by-products including free radicals and homocysteine. Vitamins strengthen the immune system, making one more resilient to disease. People with healthier bodies live longer and don't succumb to natural killers including cancer or cardiovascular diseases.

As one strives for longevity by seeking solutions to arrest aging, it is imperative that stress is controlled so it does not have an effect on one's body. Recent studies have shown that people who are continually under stress age faster. Some studies have linked high levels of cortisol in the body to stress related aging. Gideon Koren and his colleagues noted that a biological marker for physical and psychological stress can be found in hair strands. For example, cortisol levels were evaluated in the hair of patients who had heart attacks. According to Koren, the level of cortisol in hair was higher in the hospitalized sample.

Early research conducted by Martin Seligman showed that rats subjected to stress responded by exhibiting varying coping responses. Some rats sought ways of escaping from the stressor to which they had been exposed whereas others merely accepted their fate and did little other than reclining on their backs; essentially they gave up. The rats who gave up showed higher levels of corticosteroids in their blood. Corticosteroid although necessary to energize the rat under stress, is known to create a breakdown in the immune system. This research supports the notion that stress creates a build-up of a substance which is necessary but can be harmful to the physiological system.

This brings to mind early research which I conducted with patients who had suffered heart attacks and had to undergo surgery. During their recovery, these patients experienced depression and anxiety. They were later given the option of enrolling in a cognitive-behavioral counselling program. The majority who enrolled experienced relief from symptoms of depression in as little as 8 sessions of counselling. Even though they continued to experience pain in their chest because of the post-surgical healing process, they were able to regain a sense of optimism from counselling. Ostensibly this thwarted their depression which allowed them to look at life with renewed vigour.

The last piece of the longevity puzzle can be found in the research on cognitive enrichment. From the time of infancy, the brain undergoes rapid changes as the cortical neurons expand and make connections to neural pathways in the brain. Intelligence reaches its pinnacle at about age 25, when branching of the neurons is complete. Seniors must continually stimulate their brains by undertaking cognitive activities. Reading, engaging in challenging mental tasks (ie. word puzzles) or undertaking thought related activities will encourage information processing and enhance cortical activity within the brain.

One must learn to slow the ravages of time by eating better quality natural food, exercising, reducing stress, and engaging in cognitive activity. Seniors must do everything in their power to slow life's aging process. Those over the age of 50 must become proactive in their search for an elixir which will slow the aging process. Many seniors will spend time searching for answers to enhance their lives whereas others will accept their fate without a struggle to ward off the fallout of aging.

Over the past three decades I have conducted research on aging seniors. Contemplating this research, I am drawn back to a research article resting on the table. People walk briskly past but some filter into the warmth of the restaurant. A flat screened television hums in the background blurting out the stories of the day. I study the newscaster as he adjusts the microphone attached to the lapel of his dark blue sports jacket. Clearing his throat, he reads the top news items of the morning.

"The cold weather is going to continue for a few more days as the Arctic winds filter down from the north. Statistics Canada has just completed a detailed study on obesity and found 7.9 million people are overweight and 5.2 million are obese; now for the details".

Looking up at the television screen, I attempt to block the drone of the monotonic broadcast of the newsman. Occasionally his voice elevates as though he imagines someone talking louder. The newscaster seems delighted by the plight of the miserable overweight lot who from his account are actively seeking every option from surgery to new fad diets in their attempt to shed unsightly adipose tissue. The statistics are bleak. According to the data, 25 percent of the North American population will be over the age of 65 by 2032. The statistics imply that as a substantial number of seniors age, they will face physical and psychological maladies. Newscasters always seem to relish the most bleak stories of the day. It is important for one to look beyond the psychological warfare emanating from newspapers and television newscasts and search for ways of controlling the aging process.

When I first became interested in aging, my focus was on physical fitness and mental health of seniors. From my research, I found that people who exercised regularly enjoyed better emotional and physical health in their senior years. During my early career as a researcher, I explored animal models as a way of evaluating stress and its impact on behaviour. Later, I turned my focus to sports psychology and examined psychological variables and their interaction on physical fitness. This naturally led to my research interest regarding physical and psychological well-being of seniors. It is important for researchers to share this information with those who have reached the age of 50; and are heading into the final phase of their life. Erik Erikson once referred to the last phase of life as the stage of "Integrity versus Despair". By this, Erikson inferred that seniors could obtain "integrity" during their final years, if they perceived a sense of satisfaction from their life's experience. Conversely, seniors who had not obtained satisfaction in life would be left with "feelings of despair", wallowing in their misery because of failed life accomplishments.

The process of aging is a reality check. Samuel Johnston once said "knowledge on a subject is advanced because we know where to find the information." The World Wide Web has made information accessible and recent research on aging is available to those interested in seeking this knowledge. Of particular interest is the work currently being done by Al

Sears at the Wellness Research Consulting Centre in Royal Palm Beach, Florida. He has provided data on an anti-aging supplement known as TA-65 patented by TA Sciences. This drug has been administered to men between the age of 60 and 85. According to test results, after 6 months of treatment the men in the study showed stronger immune systems, improved eyesight, skin tone, and restored sex lives. The chemical basis of TA-65 is a Chinese herb known as Astragalus. This herbal medicine has apparently been used by the Chinese for centuries to offset aging. Astragalus has a positive effect on health by increasing telomerase in the cell so that it inhibits the telomeres during the process of cell division. Seniors can obtain the herbal medicine by using the raw form as the Chinese have done for centuries. Alternatively, they can purchase the drug TA-65 which has been patented by TA Sciences.

Other substances including Vitamin B2, Vitamin B6, Vitamin B12, Folic Acid, and TMG (trimethylglycine) can reduce the level of homocysteine in cells. Homocysteine build-up in the cells is contraindicated in age related disorders including heart disease, Alzheimer disease, Parkinson disease and Impotence. Substances which are also useful in offsetting aging because of their antioxidant properties include Vitamin A, Vitamin E, Vitamin C, Alpha Lipoic Acid, Coenzyme Q10, Lutein, and Lycopene. Research by Brian Clement, Director of the Hippocrates Health Institute in West Palm Beach, Florida has shown the vitamins and minerals used to enhance good health should be similar as possible to the molecular structure of those found in their natural state, because the body assimilates these much better than synthetic drugs produced in laboratories.

My early research on aging was funded by Fitness

Canada. The facts were clear, seniors who adhered to fitness programs demonstrated better physical health, less body fat distribution and more stable moods in comparison to those who didn't exercise. While perusing newspapers today, I learned that North Americans are fatter and less physically fit than they were approximately two decades prior when my aging research first commenced. According to Health Statistics, approximately 30% of adults in the USA and 20% of the adults in Canada are obese. The statistics for children and adolescents are not much better. A recent compilation of data regarding children revealed that approximately 32% in the USA and 26% in Canada were overweight. These statistics reveal a sordid state for physical health of people in North America. In comparison, the lowest obesity rates by percentage exist in Netherlands (10%), Sweden (9.7%), Denmark (9.5%), France (9.4%), Austria (9.1%), Italy (8.5%), Norway (8.3%), Switzerland (7.7%), Japan (3.2%) and South Korea (3.2%). The countries in this list have lower rates of obesity. These statistics imply that as the population ages in North America it can look forward to continued problems with obesity and the accompanying physical maladies including cardiovascular, cancer and diabetes.

As I examined the research papers spread in front of me, an elderly couple entered the restaurant and sat at the table nearby. They presented as lean and physically fit, not ravaged by the spoils of aging. I leaned into their direction, and made a comment about the weather. There is nothing better than small talk to break the barrier of silence. Introducing myself, I mentioned to the couple that I was a professor at a local university and had completed studies on aging populations. I informed them of my current research and that I was preparing a university lecture entitled "Positive Aging". The topic seemed to be of interest to the couple. They introduced themselves; George boastfully mentioned that he was 80 and his wife Emelda was 79 years of age. In his opinion, aging was a stage of life, which had positive value, only if one had a daily plan. He provided an account of the couple's planned ritual. Ostensibly, they started their day with some physical exercises, followed with a walk through the park which ended with a stop at the restaurant for a coffee. From his perspective, a routine was his "elixir" to successful aging. The elderly couple had many activities they completed before the day ended. One of their favourite events included visiting the library and browsing through the newly arrived books. They spent time reading on topics considered fascinating, this venture lasting about an hour. After their return home for a small lunch, a nap would follow. More activities would commence over the course of the afternoon and into the evening. It was George and Emelda's opinion that a life replete with activity including exercise, diet, reading and thinking was necessary for positive aging. I finished my coffee and thanked them for their insight. As I walked from the restaurant, I reflected on the idea that positive aging should include physical and cognitive activities. By listening to the opinions of seniors, one can establish a framework for appreciating the process which all seniors must undergo.

Aging has been defined as a stage, which begins with infancy and ends in senescence. During this process, one embarks on a journey of physical and cognitive change. It is during this period seniors age positively or flounder. The elixir of life appears to begin with an open mind which allows one to appreciate each event as it occurs. The activities which take place over the course of the day should challenge the body and mind. By setting daily goals, one can experience life to its fullest. For those over the age of 50, aging is of particular importance because many will reach this period and retire from the working world. After age 50 one metamorphosizes to their last stage of growth. It is during this period, life can become a fulfilling and rewarding experience.

CHAPTER ONE

THE HUMAN JOURNEY

Rule #2: To grow positively one must be adaptive.

Middle aged people I have encountered claimed their life was too stressful and they couldn't wait until they retired. After retirement, some found the pace more relaxing whereas others having had some time away from the workforce complained they were bored because they couldn't find activities to occupy their time. In this chapter, I will explore some of the concerns seniors have as they age. Some people master aging by undertaking varied activities, whereas others become anxious and distraught with their new found freedom. People are social organisms and need to interact with others. Leaving the workforce is a positive move for some, whereas others are unable to adapt to an unstructured lifestyle.

People realize that it is important to be adaptive. For those who leave their jobs, it is necessary to have other activities which will enable them to adjust to a new lifestyle. There are changes which must be undertaken if one is to be successful in their senior years. Many become carefree during this transition whereas others find themselves obsessed with minor details of their life. And some seniors cannot accept changes which occur in their lives. Cognitive and physical decline in later life make people anxious and distraught which complicates their ability to be adaptive. When people are younger, stressful events don't affect them as much because they are resilient. Life moves quickly and does not provide time to reflect on insignificant issues. Routines are followed and cognitive maps constructed to assist the individual with everyday events. As one ages, routines become of lesser importance and time fades into an abyss. Life becomes lost in a sea of time. Poor recall of familiar detail is suggestive of a deficiency in cognitive processing, an artifact of the decrement experienced during senior years.

Some research has shown that as seniors' age, they undergo changes in structure and function of the brain mechanisms. Deterioration of cells, lead to physiological and cognitive decrements. These changes can create disparaging effects to the individual who must cope with loss of mental capacity. Some agencies have patented techniques to improve one's cognitive processes through mental exercises. These can be practised on a daily basis to ensure the senior engages in cerebral tasks which assist in slowing cognitive deterioration. These exercises stimulate the mind, by engaging the neurons. They increase the processing of information as connections are made with other cortical neurons. These exercises provide the senior with stimulation of the neuronal cells. Research has shown that people who undertake cognitive activities have better thinking ability and the capacity to engage in reasoning and decision making.

Many researchers have evaluated the impact of daily exercise on physiological well-being. By undertaking physical activities including calisthenics, strength training and aerobics, oxygen is circulated to the heart and lungs which in turn conditions the body and brain. The notion of "use it or lose it" becomes the mantra of seniors who must maintain physical health so they can thwart the natural physical deterioration brought on by aging. Exercising the body becomes of importance as seniors' are faced with the challenges of physical adaptation to changing environmental situations. For the person who has reached the age of 50, loss of physical strength seems to be a challenging event. A decrement in physical ability brought on by loss in muscular strength, creates a boundary for seniors. Even the senior who has engaged in a daily regime of physical exercise will find the task of everyday activities such as opening doors difficult because they do not have the physical strength to do these tasks. Older people comment on their gratitude to mechanical engineers who devise creative techniques for automatically opening doors. The older person's life becomes easier when they are able to use modern technology.

Many seniors pursue daily workouts in fitness clubs. They report however, being challenged by physical tasks. It would seem that strength and flexibility decrease with age. Even though they perceive themselves to be young in body and mind, seniors come to the realization that they do not have the physical capacity to undertake activities they did at a younger age. Sagging muscles, wrinkled brows and traces of grey speckling the hairline are indicators of aging. After age 50, there is slow and gradual loss of physical ability because of physiological deterioration. This leads to a reduction in body strength. At the basis of this transition is the incapacity of the telomeres to divide and the inefficiency of the mitochondria to produce sufficient energy needed by the organ systems. These changes are consistent with the aging process; they become a reality for seniors.

It is difficult to be positive about aging when the older person experiences, aches, pains, diminished strength and the loss of ability to ambulate or remember things. Many people indicate they continue to feel young in their minds but when they undertake arduous tasks, they realize their body cannot handle the duress. Aging brings about physical challenges and cognitive annoyances of not remembering people or events. The fountain of youth which they search is not some drug which can be obtained in the local pharmacy, but a diet replete with its energy enhancing qualities. Seniors also require the optimism to engage in physical and cognitive activities because these assist in offsetting the challenges of everyday living.

The focus of this book is to guide the reader in savouring life's experiences and discovering the road to longevity. Maintaining an optimistic attitude is useful but not the panacea leading to successful aging. There are days when one's mood is low or a virus attacks the immune system lowering physiological resistance. This experience can be short lived if the body is replete with energy and the mind refuses to accept these negative events. The senior must fight to regain some inner balance. It is imperative that seniors practise proper dietary intake and cognitive exercises which can assist in deterring the aging process. With proper vitamins and supplements the telomeres will not deteriorate as quickly. Mind exercises including "thought stopping", a model of cognitive behavioral therapy encourages one to replace negative thoughts with positive thoughts. Seniors should not allow negative experiences to control their thoughts or emotions. Given that one takes care of their physical, emotional and mental needs, then a positive mood should prevail.

From my research, I have learned that one must challenge negative events. Physical stamina created through diet, sleep and exercise allows the senior to deal with the ongoing duress of every day problems. Mental preparation allows one to better cope. After a restful sleep, an upcoming day always appears brighter. A physically rested body allows the immune system to recharge and better handle stressors. One has to change their perception of internal thoughts if they want to change the way they will react to them.

Recently I travelled to Orlando, Florida to attend a conference. Browsing through a gift shop, a small placard suspended on the wall caught my eye. It was worded as follows: "Why worry! There are only two things to worry about; whether you are well or whether you are sick; if you are well there is nothing to worry about; if you are sick there are only two things to worry about whether you get well or whether you die; if you get well there is nothing to worry about. If you die there are only two things to worry about; whether you go to heaven or go to hell. If you go to heaven there is nothing to worry about. If you go to hell you will be so busy interacting with your friends you will have no time to worry". This statement indicates that worry is pointless. Often, people spend much of their time and energy concentrating on the negative experiences of life. Negative thinking never leads to anything but negative behaviour. These experiences can stress and weaken the immune system and lead to physical and emotional illnesses.

Impact of Stress:
Hans Selye has discussed stress in his numerous articles. Specifically, Selye was concerned with the effects of stressors on physical health. According to Selye, negative stress creates pressure on the body. The inability to control the negative stressors leads to a release of white blood cells. Eventually, the white blood cells are depleted. When the organism (animal or human) can no longer physically cope with the loss of white blood cells and a compromised immune system, it dies. The message that Selye espoused through his research was simple. It concluded that stressors create negative experiences which if not dealt with properly cause disruption to physical health, leading to exhaustion and inevitable death of the organism. Every human must have the ability to adapt to the ever changing environment. Physical, psychological and social demands create stress and these can be debilitating to one's health. One must learn to cope with these every day experiences.

The aging person has to maintain a balanced life. Physical ailments and every day maladies are important reminders that one is undergoing the aging process. Seniors who spend too much time worrying about these events will only create a negative state of mind for themselves. The imbalance in the mind and the body will lead to problems in physical and emotional health. This would infer that if you fret all of the time, you will worry yourself into an illness and imminent death.

Positive and Negative Attributes of Aging:
In comparison to negative statements, positive statements elevate one's perception of self in a useful direction. People like to associate with those who say nice things about them. These statements increase self-esteem and make others better liked. One should proceed through life with a positive attitude, this will allow for a more optimistic outlook on life. Research by Martin Seligman has shown that optimistic people do much better than pessimists following surgery. Optimists evaluate feared situations with some anxiety but at the same time attempt to look at the bright side of the negative event; specifically that their malady could be rectified through medical treatment. Research has shown that the optimistic quickly recovers following surgical procedures. Faced with an ache or pain, a person with an optimistic attitude does not take the experience out of perspective. The pain that one feels is the result of a particular event which can be overcome by correcting the problem. One must seek solutions for their ailments, rather than thinking ailments are the result of some disease which will lead to imminent death. One's focus should be on evaluating each situation in a realistic manner. Positive thoughts put ideas into perspective, whereas negative thoughts send one into panic attacks.

There is a need for seniors to question their belief system when it is negative. The idea that one can acquire cancer is certainly a reality. More people die from cancer and heart related disorders than any other physical malady. A split second self-diagnosis of cancer invading one's body founded on faulty or negative beliefs is at best a ridiculous notion. The probability of the ache being a cancer is very low indeed. In the event that one is diagnosed with cancer, the positive way of viewing this would be that recognition of the symptoms and early detection would lead to treatment. The optimistic attitude allows one to seek out remedial solutions to problems rather than fretting about the dilemma.

    The positive side of every tragic experience which one faces in life is the reality that we are mortals. Appreciating this allows us to understand that mortals have aches, pains, illnesses and the certainty that all mortals will die. The positive outlook however is the notion that many worthwhile events occur during the life cycle which can be experienced and cherished. Important events including birth, graduation, marriage, family re-unions and even death can take on some meaningfulness. In my clinical practise as a psychologist, people sometimes seek me out following the death of a loved one because of their grief. They are saddened by the death of an 80 year old parent or grandparent. To express sympathy for their loss is certainly appreciated. In these interactions, I allow the relative who is left behind to evaluate their situation so they can gain some resolution. Knowing that a loved one has achieved senior status and surpassed the life expectancy of the average person is recognized as an accomplishment. Interaction with grieved persons allows them to appreciate their deceased relative raised children, spent memorable occasions with their families, had good health for the better part of their lives and accomplished many goals. By allowing the grieved relative to focus on the positive aspects of the deceased person's life and celebrate the meaningfulness of their existence, serves to remind them that death is not merely a negative experience but part of the cycle of life.

    Birth, infancy and childhood are positive experiences; but to grow old requires patience and an effort to face life head on. The aging person must have the inner fortitude to accept the changes which come with this process. Recently, I perused an interesting research paper written by Prescott Thompson. In this article, he listed the qualities of aging. I'm not certain how the data was collected but one can probably assume the statements were gathered first hand. It is interesting to note that most of the statements made by the participants in his study were negative. The list is as follows:

1) more time alone
2) being neglected
3) having less money
4) being second best
5) giving up past lifestyle
6) loss
7) accepting help from others
8) facing death
9) living with the threat of illness or disability
10) being frightened
11) accepting past failures
12) inability to change one's past
13) trying to make sense of one's past and what it meant
14) figuring out what has to be accomplished before dying
15) having to get along with people in order to fit
16) more demand upon inner resources
17) death

There is no positive tone or enlightening aspect to this list. It would appear that Thompson's elderly population had to cope with the pressures of aging and these events left them somewhat stressed. Accepting one's failures creates stress for the person who can not change the past. People who have not accomplished their goals in life appear to get fixated on a "collective guilt" which seems to prevent them from pushing forward with their lives. The only positives that Thompson found in his research on aging included:

1) more time to do as one wants
2) greater freedom

These two factors are few in comparison to the lengthy list of negatives which seniors expressed. If one were to take the small list of positives and attempt to expand these with optimism, they could multiply significantly. The aging person has to move away from their negative experiences and not allow these to encompass their lives. By employing a positive belief system, allows one to repress the negative experiences of aging. In this way, the negative events do not become the focus of the person's daily struggles. Seniors who do not have the resources to move forward with their lives seem to engage in the stage Erik Erikson described as "despair". Some seniors need to re-focus on the factors Thompson found to be positive, specifically: 1) more time to do as one wants and 2) greater freedom.

Aging seniors must realize that a healthy body, active imagination and the drive to engage in new challenges of life, offset the negatives of ill health. The most important qualities the aging person requires are sound physical and mental health. With these two attributes the sky is the limit. One doesn't need money to engage in everyday activity. If a senior can't golf because of he/she can't afford membership fees, then they can at least drive balls on a public field or make a putting course in their back yard. One might not have a boat to go fishing but can find solace by fishing off a public pier. Others can place their names on Bulletin Boards to fish with those who have boats but no friends. There are some seniors who have boats but can't fish alone because they need assistance putting the boat in the water. The senior must become creative and find ways of fulfilling their everyday goals. The most important part of aging is to remain healthy, and that should be one's foremost pursuit. A good diet, physical and cognitive activity will assist in maintaining emotional health.

Some days as I drive to work, I notice an elderly gentleman walking along the sidewalk carrying small hand weights. As he walks briskly, he swings the weights back and forth. This is an important physical activity because it provides him with aerobic, and strength conditioning. Walking conditions his heart and cardiovascular system; and swinging of the weights, exercises his muscle tissue in his arms and legs.

My clinical practise provides me with many opportunities to counsel patients. In the following example, I will introduce you to a man who had health, finances and a stable marriage but didn't have a positive outlook on life. If he had not sought out counselling his situation could have worsened. Harry W. had attained 65 years of age and decided it was time to retire. He had worked for approximately 40 years as a chartered accountant in a private firm. Harry had fully paid for his home and had saved sufficient money for his retirement. He was in good health, had a stable marriage to a loving wife and had many friends. His hobbies included golfing, fishing, swimming and nature walks. Sometimes he pursued these alone, and at other times did them with his wife or friends. Overall, Harry's lifestyle seemed positive and could be considered acceptable to most people. Superficially, it appeared that Harry was doing okay and would live a long and healthy life. The problem however was not with Harry's pre-retirement plan but with his post-retirement plan. Harry had lived a structured lifestyle for the last forty years but he did not have a retirement plan other than spending time at his hobbies. He had no idea that retirement included structuring and organizing his day. With his week free of a 40 hour work regime, he did not have enough activities to keep himself busy throughout the day. Harry experienced anxiety because he was not content with the direction of his life. Harry often found himself bored. He ruminated frequently about his health even though he wasn't ill. In Harry's mind, he had anticipated that retirement would make him happy. Because this perceived expectancy had not reached fruition, Harry found himself spiralling toward depression. He sought out counselling because he wasn't certain how to structure his day.

  Humans are not complex individuals but do require organization and structure to make it through each day. Positive aging requires goal setting and a plan of action which will allow one to obtain their goals. The senior must be able to recognize when plans are not being fulfilled and re-adjust so that changes can be implemented. In Harry's case, he had too much time on hand after retirement. He did all the things he had not been able to do when he was employed. In the leisure of retirement, he attempted to fit all activities in but exhausted himself in the process. Finally, with little energy left, he became a fixture in his home. He interfered with his wife's lifestyle and became a problem to her. She didn't know what to do with Harry during the day when he wasn't involved with his hobbies or friends. Harry's wife began to view him as a negative stressor. She confronted Harry, and he contacted me for assistance. With counselling, Harry was able to develop a retirement plan and implement a schedule so that active days would be followed by less active days. This would enable him to rest, and plan for upcoming events. With this new improved schedule he was never bored. Through cognitive behaviour therapy, Harry W. was able to adjust his belief system to accommodate his retirement status. In time, Harry was able to re-establish a structured plan for himself and control his depressive bouts and worry.

Counselling is not prescribed as the panacea to control emotional problems, however it can provide assistance when one does not understand beneficial ways of implementing change. The individual does not always have the ability to evaluate his or her life objectively. Countless seniors like Harry W. begin retirement with a healthy attitude only to realize in a short time that retirement is not everything that it was perceived to be. Life is more than a series of activities and pleasures which can be derived from daily events. Personal obstacles prevent one from perceiving reality objectively. Being active and preoccupied, does not allow a senior to become a happier person. It is important to have plans which will engage the person and allow them to fulfil a purpose in their life.

Aging is a personal event that most people will experience at some point in their lifetime. During this time, one must have expectancies and goals. Satisfaction can be obtained from the completion of these goals but should not always be expected. The knowledge which one attains through aging is part of this process. Information which is gained from our past and present will assist in structuring the future. Seniors must recognize that life becomes an experience. They can work toward their goals and obtain some satisfaction from these accomplishments. Humans need to strive toward attainable and somewhat predicable futures. Humans are complex organisms and have particular needs. Life becomes positive if one strives toward goals that are within one's grasp. The senior should never ask what life has to offer but what they can do to make their life better.

Recently I attended a concert. The rock band was comprised of some aging musicians, well-known during the 70's era. According to their biography posted on the Web, all members were born between the 1940's and 1950's. At the time of the concert, the band members would have achieved the age of 60 to 70. One could only imagine that advanced age would have some impact on their performance on stage. Instead, the audience was treated to a rendition of memorable songs over the two hour performance. The songs conjured up images of a bygone era when life was carefree and idyllic. The voices of the band members had changed from the crisp vocals etched into the vinyl albums in my record collection, but the enthusiasm of their youth was still reflected in the lyrics.

From my research on aging, I have come to learn that with age many cognitive processes begin to fade, especially memory. This was visible in the aging rockers but the band members had learned to adjust to this demand by spreading out song sheets to cue them to the lyrics and provide direction over the course of the evening.

Physical Decrements of Aging:

According to neuroscientists, seniors lose approximately 20% of their cognitive capacity by age 60. Examples of this loss can be observed in the inability to remember names of people, important dates, or ways of doing things. Research has shown that as seniors age, the thalamus (sensory-motor relay centre located in the midline area of the brain) decreases in size. Subsequent losses are experienced in cognitive activities including verbal efficiency, memory and processing speed. These activities require an efficient thalamus. With the reduction in size of this brain structure, losses are experienced. An example of this loss can be observed in the driving behaviour of seniors. Thalamus reduction causes some seniors to drive slower and more cautiously because they lack the ability to quickly process incoming information. Recently, commentaries have appeared in the Globe and Mail on this issue. A particular article by freelance writer Lorraine Sommerfeld (January 23, 2010) pertaining to driving and the elderly, implies that as one ages, especially after age 70, there may be a need to scrutinize the driving habits of the elderly by subjecting them to driving tests to ensure they still have the capability of engaging in this activity safely.

An article by Julian Sher and Moira Welsh (February 2012), advocate for cognitive testing of seniors who want to drive their vehicles after age 70. Shawn Marshall of the Ottawa Hospital Rehabilitation Centre is currently evaluating senior drivers. From his research on the CanDrive project, he believes that many seniors have sound driving ability. He believes it is prejudical and ageist to suggest that seniors not be allowed to drive. Mark Rapoport of Toronto Sunnybrook Health Sciences Centre has found that 9000 people with dementia like conditions have been involved in automobile crashes. Furthermore, Allen Dobbs a professor emeritus of the University of Alberta is currently promoting a company known as DriveABLE. This firm has developed a two phase program. The first phase tests knowledge of driving, and the second phase evaluates road skills. This combined program will likely become a standard tool for the evaluation of senior driving ability.

If neuroscientists are accurate in claims, seniors who have lost 20% of their cognitive capacity could be affected in many pursuits including driving ability. There is a need to closely examine the senior person's driving ability to ensure they are not at risk to themselves or others while they are on the road. Many seniors over the age of 70 would easily pass the driving test whereas some would fail. An argument in favour of testing one's driving ability after age 70 would be to ensure added safety to those who use the roadways. But at the same time, this would provide reassurance to those in the community that by age 70, many seniors still have the ability to function well at this task.

The decrement in processing speed in seniors can be delayed as long as one continues to engage in physical tasks (ie. exercise, or hands on activities) and cognitive tasks (ie. reading, thinking and decision making). Many physical activities including walking and everyday performance tasks can enhance one's sensory and motor processing ability and reduce physical decline. A person who is engaged in physical activity assumes control of their motor skills. Seniors who are actively using sensory-motor and cognitive skills, retain their brain in a high state of preparedness. In essence, the elixir for positive aging would imply that by undertaking a multitude of tasks including proper dietary intake, physical activity and intellectual challenges could assist in slowing the process of aging. Life continues after age 50, however the power of fruitful aging can only occur if the body and mind remain active. Ongoing exercise, cognitive challenges, proper nutrition and a positive attitude will allow the senior to prosper.

Aging is a stage of life, the budding infant blossoms into a flowering adolescent, and the young adult arrives at middle age ready to metamorphosize into a healthy senior. The period from age 50 until senescence, is the last stage of life and initiates a starting point and the focus of this book. By age 50, one has completed a significant cycle of life. The senior has many experiences from which they can reflect. If one could gaze into a crystal ball, it might provide a rendition of the events found in the life cycle. To grow old is a fact of life. And some do not look forward to the process of aging. One senior reflected in her musings that senescence was not the "golden age" which had been described during her middle years. According to this lady, there was nothing "golden" about the physical maladies which came with old age. Aging she reflected, was more about the memories which she could glean from her past and these memories provided meaning for her current existence. By reminiscing about distant events, she could draw from her past and find the courage needed to face the future.

Seniors have mentioned that memories recorded on old photographs can take them back to the place and time of their birth. The memories are distant, but if one can explore these thoughts, the images will flow forward to a present state of consciousness. To many, memories provide a sense of comfort. From these treasures, the events recounted from an earlier period renew one's vigour for life. The sentinel in all of us guards memories for later reflection. Past events are retained in the woven fabric of our lives. These events provide meaning and strengthen the knowledge of our roots. However, one doesn't know how our lives will end. There is no elixir which makes the meaning of life any sweeter, only the memories which find their resting place in the omnipresent. The meaning of life is the recognition that senescence will be an eventful period. The meaning of one's existence can be drawn from the distant past. Memories provide us with some hope for our future. It is not the length of time which one lives, but the ability to live and cherish each day. Memories are created by daily events and stored in our brains to remind us of our well travelled journey. These events will sustain the aging person into senescence and will bear fruit for later reflection.

An examination of historical data can provide much information regarding one's longevity. Companies have sprung forth to evaluate one's DNA to provide an understanding of ancestral longevity. The original Genome project has done much to provide knowledge of the past. One can seek out a company engaged in this pursuit and by submitting a sample of DNA (ie. blood or saliva) data bases can be searched for one's ancestral roots.

There are many uncertainties in life. By looking beyond the present, one can obtain some insight of the positive aspects of aging. The meaning of life is not found on some distant shore but savoured by each moment of one's existence. Each day should be relished with the distinct flavour of the activities which fabricate one's personal dictionary of life. This can provide meaning to one's existence and make aging nothing but a stage. Through the eyes of seniors, one can gain some perspective on the aging process. Through self-reflection, seniors can obtain some insight into their aging process.

Only 5000 years prior, the average life expectancy was short and people who reached age 30 were considered old. Today, according to Statistics Canada one can achieve an average existence of 80 years. Medical science has expanded one's existence by conquering diseases which lead to premature death. But one's fountain of youth is limited and eventually time runs out for the living. Life will come to an end as abruptly as it started. Regardless of the pursuits made by medical science, our time on earth is coded in the genes, life style and the diseases of modern day society. There is no easy answer to the mystery of longevity. Having some control of our lives however, can be of some comfort to the human psyche. Conversely, having prior knowledge of the time of one's death would only create overwhelming anxiety and fear. This would interfere with the way one conducted their everyday affairs and prevent the individual from enjoying their existence. Human beings can achieve some meaning from life and this potential can be measured through tangible experiences. These experiences can't always be evaluated extrinsically but one must look for intrinsic answers.

Summary and Conclusions:
In writing this book, I have interacted with many people over the age of 50. They have provided me with some insight regarding the aging journey. The most important point which I have gleaned from my interaction with seniors is that successful aging is not about the number of years one achieves but the contentment derived from each daily experience. The commonality found amongst the many articles which I have

read on aging is the notion that one cannot control every moment of life but only savour it as it transpires. Many people over the age of 50 seem intent on achieving longevity. During this stage, they hope to accomplish their goals and fulfil their experiences.

With the advancement of science and medicine, the upper limit of life will only increase with the passage of time. By the year 2100, average life expectancy could possibly exceed 100 years. It is not the number of years which one obtains out of life but the worthwhile experiences achieved. Many seniors concur, physical and mental health become important measures of their well-being. Seniors who achieve age 50 and older, agree that life is only of importance as long as emotional health is intact. Seniors fear physical maladies because these can lead to impairment and institutionalization. A lengthy life cycle is only of importance to the senior who has sound mental and physical health. For middle aged persons, there is an interest in maximizing one's time on earth through the pursuit of healthy activities. Those who age positively, find themselves seeking ways of maximizing their life rather than reflecting on the negative events which lead to an early demise. Many people over the age of 50, do not believe it serves any importance to concentrate on the negative issues but instead prefer to envision a period of growth where retirement will provide them with a meaningful existence. Healthy people concentrate on positive attributes. Life is short and from a pragmatic point of view, one realizes from the time of birth, aging begins. One must permit their left cerebral cortex of their brain to control the feelings generated by the emotionality of their right cerebral cortex. It is best not to allow the right brain to override the logic of the left brain. Psychologists have shown from their research, right brain dominant people including artists and writers are more prone to emotionally labile experiences including depression or bipolar mood conditions. There is nothing wrong with emotional experiences, but when the emotions are too frequent and too severe and interfere with life, there is a propensity for the aging person to spend too much time engaged in labile experiences. Rather than enjoying the positive aspects of their lives, people spend too much time reflecting on the low points of their existence and find themselves anxious, fearful and fixated on these negative experiences. Misery loves miserable company and despondency, gloom and depression co-exist as friends.

Life is cast as a linear event. It has a beginning and it has an end. One can not ask to get off the "cycle of life". Aging continues whether or not the person is content with the choices they have made. Introspection is useful because it allows for an examination of everyday events. It permits one to look into their inner self. From self-analysis, the meaning of life can be obtained from one's existence. Life has a beginning and by concentrating on the benefits of this starting point, one can obtain insight into the positive aspects. The birth of an infant is undeniably one of the most pleasurable events experienced by parents. Watching a child grow provides a sense of comfort to parents and hope for the future of the family. Birth is viewed with this singular notion and represents the positive aspect of life. Birth is seen as a renewable resource, something good and beneficial and the infant representative of the symbolism.

A philosophical evaluation of aging leads one to acknowledge the notion that life is short. Birth and death can be viewed as the extreme ends of this continuum. Eastern philosophies describe these as consistent with the "Yin and the Yang" or balance found during the life process. Life is not always comprised of positives but every person can derive positive meaning from the paradox of birth and death, and search for some meaning along this road. The fact a person is born, ages and dies does not seem too inspirational and can cast some gloom. I talked with one aging person who had just turned 70. He reflected the tragedy of life was the fact that he spent so much time learning, only to have this knowledge lost with his death. Knowledge however does not have to be lost with death, but must be passed on to the younger generation.

Life as we know it on earth has a beginning, to grow positively means to accept the things which happen and make the best of this process. The views expressed in this book will not attempt to evaluate the mysteries of evolution, creation nor focus on a spiritual context. Instead, my focus will be to explore the individual experience and examine a scientific perspective. This should allow the senior to gain some understanding of the aging process. Aging positively is about mind over matter, and this is the human journey one must travel to ensure a valuable existence after age 50.

Abraham Maslow a prominent humanist in the field of psychology believed that humans were motivated by biological and social needs. He believed humans prioritize these on a continuum. Initial goals include physiological, safety, security and love needs. Once these are attained, humans seek to fulfil their esteem, understanding and aesthetic needs. Finally when all needs are accomplished, the senior person can become self-actualized. This infers that one can obtain fulfilment once they have reached their potential. Much like positive aging, self-actualization is the realization that life plans have been achieved. A reflection of one's past during the senior years provides the individual with the knowledge that goals have been accomplished. The senior must reflect on the past and use this to create a plan for the future.

CHAPTER TWO

THE PHYSIOLOGICAL BASIS OF AGING

Rule #3: One can increase physiological stamina through diet, sleep and exercise.

Alexander Leaf and John Launois wrote an article entitled "Every Day is a Gift when You are Over 100". This was featured in the National Geographic, January 1973 edition. In this interesting evaluation of centenarians, the authors wrote "there is no known gene for longevity, only the absence of bad genes". These researchers studied elderly people in three remote mountainous regions; the Andean Village of Vilcabamba, Ecuador; the Hunza in the Karakoram Range in Kashmir; and the Abkhazia in the Georgian Soviet Socialist Republic. Many centenarians who resided in these regions were well beyond the age of 100. The elixir to their longevity appeared to be genetic, diet and physical activity. Their daily lives were replete with physically rigorous activity and a good diet. Resting blood pressure for many of these centenarians was below 120/80, the normal systolic /diastolic standard. Furthermore, the evaluation of centenarians who resided in the regions showed caloric intake of 1200 to 2000 per day. In contrast, a 1968 study by the U.S. National Academy of Sciences had shown that people over the age of 55, males in particular should ingest 2400 calories whereas females should ingest 1700 calories. In 1973 researchers found Americans of all ages ingested 3300 calories per day. Not only did the Americans eat considerably more food than required for healthy living, and also consumed the wrong types of foods.

A comparison of the three regions studied by Leaf and Launois showed that only 12 to 60 grams of fat were consumed on a daily basis, the majority originating from vegetable sources. Genetics and diet appeared to play a significant part in longevity of the centenarians studied. It appeared that only "good genes" had been passed through generations to the inhabitants of these three regions. It would be of interest for present day researchers to revisit these same regions to re-evaluate the inhabitants. This would provide an ongoing synopsis of the impact of modern times and its effect on diet, physical activity and changing lifestyles. It would also be interesting to learn whether the centenarians in the early 1970's study are still healthy and alive today.

Earlier, I presented some research which indicated the primary emphasis of sound aging could be found in a person's DNA. A quick evaluation can be made of one's DNA by studying the lineage of paternal and maternal ancestors. If both sides of one's family are comprised of ancestors who have aged well, there is a good chance longevity is consistent within the gene pool of that family. An exciting discovery by Paola Sebastiani a biostatistician, and Thomas Perls a gerontologist has shown that a DNA sample using 150 genetic markers can reveal with 77% accuracy whether one will live to 100. At one time, it was believed that humans had approximately 100,000 genes located on the arms of the 23 pairs of chromosomes. Scientific evidence now shows that humans only have about 20,000 to 30,000 genes. These hold the basic code for longevity, in time the genetic markers predicting illness may be scientifically altered to reduce the disease process.

It is just a matter of time before researchers find the basis of longevity. In his November 10, 2010 newsletter Al Sears discussed the basis of women's greater longevity in comparison to men. Statistics show that women live approximately 4 years longer than men in North America. Spanish researchers have found that women's longevity may be a result of the "Methuselah enzyme" (Methuselah is the Old Testament character who apparently lived 969 years). Apparently the basis of this super enzyme lies in a chemical referred to as superoxide dismutase. This enzyme reduces superoxide, the most common free radical in the body. As a person ages, the proportion of free radical levels in the body increase while superoxide dismutase decreases. Ostensibly superoxide dismutase consists of two sub-types. One has a copper/zinc basis and the other a manganese basis. Copper/zinc superoxide dismutase reduces the aging process by protecting cell cytoplasm whereas manganese superoxide dismutase protects mitochondria from being damaged by free radicals. Since both of these processes lead to better cell durability, superoxide dismutase is necessary to create longevity for the cell and boosting the body's immune system. In the future, this chemical will likely be produced synthetically and administered to increase longevity in the aging population.

Impact of Telomeres and Telomerase on Longevity:
An investigation by Geraldine Aubert and Peter Lansdorp has shown that at the basis of good aging are telomeres. The evidence indicates that each time a cell divides, telomeres shorten. The cells can only divide a limited number of times before they die. According to Leonard Hayflick most cells divide about 80 times before they eventually deteriorate; this notion is referred to as the Hayflick Limit. Personal communication with Kabwe Nkongolo, a geneticist at Laurentian University would indicate that in order to age well, one should have an abundance of hardy long strand telomeres and have the added activity of telomerase, an enzyme which inhibits the telomeres from deterioration as the cell divides. This cellular activity seems to be at the basis of longevity of the cell. Research shows that seniors whose cells divide with the least amount of deterioration tend to have better capability of aging best. Conversely, seniors with telomeres that shorten with each cell division because of limited telomerase are more at risk for quicker deterioration. The more divisions a cell undergoes the greater the loss in telomere length and subsequently a propensity toward cell death. Cells are at the basis of all organ systems and in time will deteriorate thereby leading to aging. The basis of longevity therefore can be scientifically evaluated by examination of the genes and altered via genetic engineering or through the use of enzymes such as superoxide dismutase which prevent free radicals from damaging cells.

For longevity to occur cells should have telomeres with long strands and an abundance of telomerase; this will assist in arresting the process of cell and organ deterioration. Seniors with telomeres that withstand cell division are more likely to age slower. It appears that some people are luckier than others by inheriting the right genetics. Over the course of this chapter, I will evaluate many facets of the physiological process of aging and its impact on cognition, memory and intelligence. Research has found that some people will be more resilient in these domains providing them with an added benefit during the aging process.

During middle age (ie. 40-60 years), adults become aware of their physical and bodily changes and adjust their lifestyle so they can better cope. Many seniors maintain balance in their daily activities while others actively seek out new diets or exercise programs to assist in the pursuit of good health. Research has shown that seniors who adopt healthy diets, physical fitness programs, become more socially and cognitively active. The research has also shown some interesting findings:

1) exercise strengthens telomeres.
2) the enzyme telomerase, prevents deterioration of the telomeres.
3) the natural substance, astragalus increases the activity of telomerase in the cell.
4) superoxide dismutase assists in removing free radicals from the cells.These discoveries will be of importance for those studying the process of aging. They may indeed become the panacea in our search for increasing longevity.

Neuronal Changes and Cognitive Growth:
Sidney Segalowicz and Patricia Davies have shown from their research that physiological changes in the body are ongoing from birth, but the greatest acceleration appears during adolescence. Apparently neurons undergo dendritic arborization as the brain accelerates in growth during the adolescent stage with peaking in neuronal growth at about age 13, age 15 and age 18. A number of cognitive changes occur in the frontal brain as dendrites branch out and make connections with other neurons. After age 20, the brain has made most of its neuronal connections and the young adult reaches the highest level of cognitive processing/intelligence at age 25. By this time most of the neural networks have been formed in the brain. The young adult is now prepared for cognitive challenges. The cerebral cortex has some plasticity, which infers the cortex is malleable and can adapt to novel changes brought about by aging or injury.

An evaluation of the aging process can be done through longitudinal research. For example, if one collected baseline data including intellectual and cognitive abilities at age 25, information would be available for later comparison. Researchers who collect data on intellectual ability, memory, verbal reasoning and processing reaction time, would have a way of comparing the changes which occur over a person's life. It is important to remember that people reach their pinnacle of intelligence at age 25. One doesn't get any smarter after this age but can retain their level of intellect by engaging in cognitive activities. Some make a point of evaluating their height and weight on a regular basis especially if they pursue physical fitness at a gym, but many do not evaluate ongoing cognitive abilities. The cognitive and physical changes which occur in later life especially after age 50 would provide the senior with a way of understanding the impact of these changes on cognitive processing. It is important to have an empirical basis for evaluating physiological changes especially when maladies occur during later years.

A collection of life's milestones, including intellectual and physical could prove of some medical benefit. The longitudinal model of research allows the senior to understand the physiological changes which they undergo as they age. From a pragmatic point, this could prove to be of some importance. By having access to their personal data in the event one succumbs to physical ailments (ie. Alzheimer, Parkinson, Cerebral Vascular Accidents or Dementia), could prove to be of merit. For example, psychological testing which evaluates intelligence, cognition, and memory at age 50 would provide a "time capsule" whereby information would be available for later comparison. This medical information could provide useful data to the individual who may want to evaluate the physiological changes which have occurred at age specific intervals (ie. 50; 60; 70; 80; 90; 100 years). Knowing one's intellectual quotient through the use of the Wechsler Intelligence Scale, would allow the senior to understand the changes which occur in reasoning, processing speed and decision making as one ages. If by chance, the senior experienced some physical or cognitive impairment in later life, an accurate comparison could be made. With data collected from other psychometric tests including the Wechsler Memory Scale (ie. general, logical, immediate and delayed memory) a detailed record would be available.

If one is lucky enough to attain centenarian status, then it would be useful to understand the changes which have occurred over a life time. Having historical data would allow the senior some information which could be shared with their physician. The physician could then ascertain changes which may have occurred following disease, accident or via the aging process. This would serve as a good guideline for diagnostic and prognostic care. Research has shown that most people undergo cognitive changes between 60 to 100 years of age. Apparently some will naturally lose up to 20% of their cognitive capacity by age 60, and 40% by the time they are 80 years of age. The loss of cognitive ability however is greatly reduced in seniors who continue to challenge their brains by engaging in new tasks as they age. For example, research collected on active academics who on a daily basis prepared notes, read articles or conducted research, showed they fared better intellectually than people who did not engage in cognitive activities. The notion of "use it or lose it" would apply to those persons who fail to undertake new cognitive challenges as they age.

In my clinical practise, I have assessed patients with myriad mental, emotional and cognitive difficulties. It is the evaluation of older patients however that has proved challenging. I recall a case of a female patient who was referred to my office at age 65 because she was experiencing memory difficulties. This woman had been an administrator at a hospital. She was referred for cognitive and memory evaluation after reporting to her physician that she was constantly forgetting things. Her main concern was the inability to remember details of immediate activities. For example, after departing from her home she would obsessively ruminate whether she had turned off the stove or locked the door. Often, she would abort her trip and return home to ensure everything was in order. As she discussed her personal concerns pertaining to memory, I hypothesized that her difficulties could be a result of cognitive and/or memory decline. This type of decline is often found in senior persons. This client presented as a perplexed, anxious person who ruminated that she might be showing early signs of Alzheimer disease. She was frightened and agitated by her cognitive status and wanted some answers pertaining to her current memory dilemma. It was her concern that in time, she would have to be hospitalized because of problems with her memory. Furthermore, this patient queried whether her poor memory was only a component of more extensive deterioration which would eventually lead to confinement in a senior's facility.

Cognitive assessment with the Wechsler Adult Intelligence Scale showed this lady was functioning in the average range of cognition but she had some weakness in auditory and visual memory. A further evaluation using the Wechsler Memory Scale showed that she was functioning below average on immediate memory and delayed memory recall. Overall, these weaknesses would pose some problems. At the time of the assessment, I didn't have access to any historical data especially a past psychological assessment of this patient's intellectual and/or memory capacity. One must remember, this patient had functioned in a high level position as an administrator in a hospital. One could surmise that she had been a bright person with good organizational skills to have functioned in her demanding role. The results of the assessment however, could not provide me with a comparison of her cognitive ability throughout her middle years (ie. age 25 to age 60). In other words, I had no baseline data, nor any way of knowing what her I.Q. or memory scores were when she was younger. The data collected at age 65 did not provide me with clear insight regarding the cognitive changes which may have occurred over a 35 year period.

As noted earlier, people are at the highest level of intellectual ability at age 25. If the aforementioned patient had been previously assessed and had provided me with her earlier baseline data, I would have had a more accurate way of diagnosing her problems. I was able to inform this 65 year old patient of her current cognitive status and her memory scores. Furthermore, I was able to provide her with the normative data. I informed this patient she should return to my office for further evaluation in 6 to 12 months so that I could re-evaluate her cognition and memory. Future data collection would provide me with an understanding of progressive cerebral changes. Only in this way, would I have the ability to state with certainty that she was showing significant cognitive decrement.

Providing patients with an accurate diagnosis of their cognitive or memory impairment, has to include two sets of data, one prior to the disorder and one following the onset of the disorder. The main crux of this chapter is to focus on the physiological changes which happen from middle to later senescent years. Many scientific studies have been completed on the elderly. The results show that not all elderly persons show the same degree of physical deterioration over time. Those with sound genetic make-up show greater longevity whereas others with deficient genetics succumb to the ravages of aging. Natural deterioration and disease will eventually have a deleterious impact on the senior person. By having some knowledge of one's genealogy and the medical problems experienced by one's ancestors will give rise to a better understanding of the familial aging process.

Physiological aging is not always positive. As one approaches middle age, organ systems begin to show signs of wear and tear. This is due in part to the deterioration of the telomeres and destruction of the cells within the organ systems. Cells are the basic building blocks of the organs. With aging, the mitochondria in each cell of the body become less efficient. The senior person only begins to realize the extent of the aging process as the body begins to deteriorate. Research by Bruce Ames and fellow researchers at University of California, have found cell destruction commences with the natural deterioration of mitochondria. The mitochondria are organelles found within cells. Ostensibly their main function is to convert sugar, fatty acids and amino acids into energy. The energy is then consumed by the cell so that it can engage in its everyday function. With the aging process, the mitochondria degenerate and undergo oxidation leaving the cells less efficient. With deterioration of these mitochondrial cells, the organ systems eventually malfunction.

In practical terminology, this means that with aging, the cells are no longer able to carry out the same level of function they were capable of doing when the person was younger. Not only do the organ systems (ie. heart, liver, lungs) show impairment but also the nervous system and the immune system malfunction. When the immune system deteriorates, pathogens including viruses and bacteria invade the organ systems. From a physiological perspective, this is disastrous because the eventual result is destruction, failure and loss of organ function. With the diminution of bodily processes, impairment of the brain and spinal cord follow. Many elderly people have healthy bodies and the right set of genes to delay the aging process. Inevitably however, one's organ systems will fail and the senior person dies of what is termed "natural causes".

The average life expectancy for humans of the 2000's is approximately 80 years. There is a slight variation for gender, with females having a lengthier age span than males. Life expectancy however will continue to increase with scientific and technological advancements. Aging infers that the human organism can maintain a "healthy physiological status" until the natural process of deterioration shuts down the body's ability to function. Humans can achieve a lengthy life expectancy under the right conditions; longevity is not written in stone. Research would indicate that lifestyle which includes proper diet, exercise and rest are instrumental for longevity. In infancy, there is a rapid expansion of the cognitive and physiological processes. By age 25, physiological maturity has been achieved and from this point onward the changes which occur in the body are a function of genetic variability and lifestyle of the human organism.

Commencing with young adulthood until the middle adult years, most of us are busy with daily activities. We take little time to evaluate the lifestyle we are pursuing and often forget the importance of diet, exercise and rest. To fulfil our work schedule and extracurricular activities, some bypass the importance of proper diet, settling for "fast foods" which are loaded with saturated fats. Coupled with this is lack of sleep, which according to Census Canada is about 6 hours nightly instead of the 8 hours needed for restorative function of bodily processes. People are so actively engrained in their lives, they take little time to evaluate their style of living.

After age 50 as one approaches retirement, many

become aware of the impact of lifestyle. The senior person becomes cognizant of particular details including the recognition they are overweight and in poor physical condition. They begin to re-evaluate their life in an attempt to change the physiological damage they have accrued. Once diet and exercise are inculcated into the senior person's life, then an attempt can be made to cultivate activities and establish priorities. The schemata of life would include devising priorities including hobbies, recreational pursuits and activities which create a physiological balance. In this way, one can minimize stress so that it does not interfere with the pituitary-adrenocortical axis. Under stress, the body releases high levels of cortisol into the blood. High cortisol interferes with the protective function of the immune system; this hormone antagonizes and depletes the white blood cells necessary for warding off pathogens.

The Progression of Aging:
Research has shown that specific changes occur in thinking, memory, intelligence and sensory-motor systems during the aging process. With aging and cell deterioration, cognitive processing is diminished. Interaction with seniors can provide a first hand account of the many challenges experienced by the aging person. In conversation with those over age 50, it becomes apparent that some individuals lose their flow of information and exhibit a rather abrupt halt in conversation as they forget the content of their thoughts. This can serve as a marker that information processing is beginning to deteriorate. For example, research by Dana Murphy and colleagues found older adults were less efficient than younger adults at

remembering information in "two person conversations". The age related decline in tracking conversation according to Dana Murphy and colleagues would indicate one's perception of information decreases. This is somewhat disconcerting for the older person, thereby creating frustration when they find themselves lost in a conversation. To compensate, the senior person searches for the context of the conversation but is unable to express their opinions. Confabulation sometimes occurs and this allows one to compensate for the memory loss. The loss of ability to track properly in a conversation is a direct result of the deterioration of information as it enters the sensory systems (ie. ears or eyes) and enters the hippocampus, the encoding centre required for immediate or short-term memory recall. All sensory information is processed through the hippocampus before it is passed to the brain where it is translated into some meaningful piece of information.

Humans process numerous bits of information every day. This information allows the person to sense and perceive the world around them. It allows the person to make meaningful responses to incoming information. Joel Myerson and her colleagues believe processing of information is a complex task which requires a series of steps. First, information must be processed in discrete stages. At the onset, the incoming bits inundate the sensory systems. To complicate matters, some information is lost during the initial stage of encoding and integration into the sensory system. The elderly person requires more time to make sense of the information because of their less efficient physiological system. This leads to a greater amount of time needed for inputting, analyzing and outputting the response. For example, take a situation in which the elderly person is doing price comparison in a grocery store. Before making a decision, the unit price of the item would be scanned visually so the sensory receptors could encode the information into the brain. One has to evaluate many factors including memories of past purchases and deduce whether the item in question is good value by unit price. This can be a difficult situation for even the cognitively astute who must evaluate different levels of information. For those people who are up in age, this may create a cognitive strain.

The senior who frequently engages in mental mathematical computations because they enjoy shopping, would not have a difficult time with the analytical process of comparative shopping. However, seniors who do not engage in this activity often, nor enjoy this activity would have a more difficult time with this task. The experience known as "use it or lose it" is a function of the level of ongoing cognitive activity undertaken by the cerebral cortex (brain). Lack of usage of the brain causes the central nervous system (ie. the sensory/motor nerves and neurotransmitters) to slowly deteriorate. With diminished cognitive usage, information processing becomes an arduous task. With the passage of time, memory is altered and this causes the senior person to falter at novel tasks. Research by Raymond Cattell has shown that "crystallized intelligence", the long term storage of old information is much better in seniors than "fluid intelligence", the ability to engage in new tasks.

Joel Myerson and colleagues make it quite clear that younger persons use the same steps of information processing as the older person. The older person however requires more time in processing information. This is somewhat consistent with the notion put forth by Jack Botwinick who found that elderly people tend to be more cautious and therefore take longer to respond to information than younger people. The main point that emerges here is that older people can sense and perceive just as well as younger people given they take adequate care of their sensory receptors (ie. wear corrective lenses or use hearing aids) and tackle mental/cognitive challenges on a routine basis. They may however need more time to complete the processing of information.

Cognitive Aging:
As one ages, deterioration of the body occurs as a natural process. There is a tendency for the organ systems to break down. The wear and tear of everyday living combined with natural genetic deterioration is at the basis of this process. There is evidence to infer that neurons in the frontal brain, where thinking and reasoning occur, are lost as early as the fourth decade of life. Research by Denise Park would indicate that the greatest problem faced by baby boomers in the 21st century is cognitive decline, this being a number one health concern.

A close evaluation of the physiological processes would indicate that blood has to be pumped through the heart and blood vessels. An improper diet, especially one high in carbohydrates and polysaturated fats can result in the clogging of blood vessels. A constriction of the arteries known as arteriosclerosis, places a greater demand on the heart. In turn, this organ works harder to deliver oxygen, vitamin and mineral by-products to the cells of the body. With deterioration of the cardiovascular system and a decrease in the lung output, a breakdown occurs in the organ systems. As oxygen supply is reduced to the brain, neurons deteriorate. The resultant effect is a decrement in the brains ability to perform tasks efficiently. Not only is thinking diminished but also encoding, storage and retrieval of memory are impaired.

According to medical experts, deterioration of the organ systems can be greatly reduced if the senior person maintains good physical health. Apparently, cognitive health can be improved through a variety of methods including diet, undertaking challenging mental tasks, engaging in hands on activities and by pursuing hobbies (ie. chess, checkers, and/or cards) which challenge thinking strategies. These mental activities increase the flow of information at the neuron and allow for greater activity at dendritic synapses. In turn, the cerebral activities increase the cognitive processing of information. Some health experts believe that deprived environments may not provide the proper stimulation necessary to encourage advanced cognitive functioning. For example, seniors who spend countless hours watching non-educational television do not have sufficient cognitive enrichment to increase higher level thinking. Over time, these seniors show decrements in thinking ability. Warner Schaie believes daily participation in mental and physical activities is associated with better performance on intelligence tests. Laura Baker has added that older adults who had mild cognitive impairment showed improvement in executive function after 6 months if they became involved in aerobic exercises four days per week. Denise Park's research using neuroimaging indicated that new neural pathways could be created in the frontal lobes of aging individuals who engaged in physical tasks.

Some studies have also shown that seniors who were disengaged and were not involved in any form of activity (social or physical) showed the greatest decrement in cognitive performance. Many investigators agree that an active lifestyle increases cognitive processing in seniors. By consistently engaging in tasks, the brain becomes more efficient and is able to process verbal information, word meaning, and comprehension of stimuli. Peter Houx and Jelle Jolles have found that amongst healthy older people with no history of biological disorder or psychiatric complications, reaction time to a task is slower when comparisons are made with their younger counterparts. Faster reaction in thought processing requires fluid intelligence. This type of thinking flows from the frontal lobes of the brain. The aging process apparently reduces the fluid ability of older people. As the senior person ages, more time and energy is required to complete tasks. This would imply that seniors need to cognitively challenge themselves daily so they remain sharp and mentally ready for incoming information. Rather than avoiding a new challenge, the senior person must embrace this as a necessary means of maintaining or increasing their cognitive ability.

Intelligence and Aging:
Seniors interviewed in my past research have indicated their greatest concern as they age, pertains to decrement in physical health and intellectual skills. Physical health has been defined as the integration of the bodies' internal organs (ie. brain, heart, lungs, liver, kidneys, and the immune system) and skeletal musculature system (ie. bones and muscles). The ability of the organ systems to work cohesively allows for a full range of thought, internal activities and body movements. If the senior person has these capacities then he or she

will have the ability to enjoy their later years. Research by Warner Schaie indicates middle aged adults must engage in ongoing cognitive challenges for their intelligence to be maintained at an optimal level. Generally, decrements in intelligence are slight for one between the age of 40 to 60. After age 60 however, particularly in those seniors who do not involve themselves in challenging cognitive activities, there is a natural and slow decrement in intelligence. The decrement is dependent upon one's everyday social engagement, learning and the challenges they expose themselves during this period. Research has shown that individuals involved in intellectually challenging pursuits show a slower decline in intellectual ability. Conversely, those who do not challenge themselves cognitively and only engage in non-active tasks (ie. watching television) have a greater decrease in intellectual ability. Richard Charter and Apostolos Alekoumbides indicate from their research, that a decrement in intelligence is most pronounced by the time a person reaches age 80. They found that as the senior person matures, special techniques must be used to compensate for their lack of efficiency. These include cognitive strategies which allow for better organization of daily life activities. For example, if the senior has a difficult time remembering where they had placed their door keys, a strategy (ie. hanging them on a key board beside the door) would be implemented to assist in circumventing this problem. The senior is encouraged to return the keys to the "Key Board" after every usage.

Memory of the Senior Person:
Roger Dixon and his colleagues have found that all forms of memory do not deteriorate at the same rate. For example, episodic memory which refers to experienced events, specifically trying to remember the names of people, where one parked their car or a conversation, shows a quick decline amongst seniors. Even though this is the last of the memory systems to develop, it is the first to deteriorate. Conversely, semantic memory which is the acquisition and retention of facts and general knowledge is the last to go. When older people are evaluated on tests which measure this, they do well at these tasks. Research would indicate that seniors tend to show greater deficits in recent memory (short term recall) than distant memory (long term recall). Furthermore, seniors show poorer recall than younger people on general memory tasks. Fergus Craik and Donald Struss have noted certain types of memory tend to decline faster in seniors. These include working memory (reasoning and problem solving), autobiographical memory (recall of everyday events), and prospective memory (the completion of activities). Research by Joan Erber and her colleagues has shown that seniors with a mean age of 71 years were less apt to get upset with memory failure than younger adults with a mean age of 24 years. Senior adults tend to accept memory decrements as they age. Tolerance of memory decrement becomes expected as a natural process of aging. Personal expectations can assist one in coming to terms with the negative impact of memory deterioration. Other researchers have found that seniors with previous good memories tend to be more depressed when they lose their memory potential. The important point one has to realize is that with aging, one must reduce their

personal expectations. Life does not always provide positive outcomes. To age gracefully infers one has to be willing to accommodate changes as they occur.

My initial research into the area of memory started about 1974 when I was a graduate student. At that time, I was involved in experimental research evaluating memory mechanisms in lower organisms (rats). Of special concern was the internal cognitive-memory mechanism which allowed the rats to inhibit their actions. A study by Bert Sombrutski and myself showed the hippocampus was responsible for encoding and storage of information. In our research project, we taught rats to perform a task through operant conditioning (ie. food reward for performance) and then later surgically destroyed the posterior and medial sections of the hippocampus, a specialized area of the brain necessary for the storage of memories. Our research findings indicated that following the destruction of the hippocampus, rats weren't able to retain their recall of previously learned events. In conclusion, it was our belief the hippocampus played an instrumental role in encoding information. Damage to the hippocampus, prevented the rats from remembering information when they were later re-tested. This finding seems to be of importance to human research. The results would indicate that once the hippocampus deteriorates because of accident, disease or via the aging process, there is little one can do to renew its ability to encode and/or remember new information.

Cognitive Decline and Memory:
An examination of the literature on memory loss has shown that seniors are not as efficient at short-term memory tasks.

This would imply that seniors who undertake the learning of a new task require more time to learn the fundamentals of this operation. Research also shows that a senior's crystallized memory (long-term recall) is just as good as that of their younger counterparts. Ysbrand Van Der Werf and colleagues found that as one ages, there is a decrease in the size (volume) of the thalamus. The thalamus' main role is that of attention, arousal and processing of information. The thalamus serves as a relay mechanism by sending incoming sensory information to other brain structures. With aging, the thalamus decreases in size. The concomitant loss of processing speed and diminution of cognitive processing in the aging senior occurs because of the thalamus' deterioration.

For the most part, seniors are not always cognizant of the changes in their memory as they age. There are numerous incidents in one's life which create conflict but these are not always viewed as problematic. I can recall a fellow university professor who was employed in my department some years prior. He had achieved the age of 60 and his memory was beginning to fade. This man was not completely aware of the changes that were occurring to him. He started having problems with his recent and delayed memory to the point they were beginning to impact on his daily life as a professor. His loss in memory is orchestrated in the following example. My vehicle was being repaired. My professor friend offered to give me a ride to a local auto repair shop so that I could retrieve my car. We left the department and walked toward the parking lot. For approximately five minutes we searched for his vehicle and then in a somewhat confused and embarrassed manner, he stated that his wife must have given him a ride to the university. He stated that his wife had probably gone on some errands and would return later, to retrieve him. Often older people fail to recognize the frailty of their memory but when an incident of retrieval failure occurs they attempt to use compensatory methods including defense mechanisms (ie. rationalization) to protect themselves from embarrassment. Many people succumb to memory loss during their lives, but for the senior this becomes problematic. The following example serves as another incident involving memory loss in an aging professor. Professor Henry had worked for many years at the university at both the administrative and departmental level. One day I met him walking toward the psychology department's secretarial office. He struggled for a few minutes as he attempted to unlock the door. I was surprised by his actions because he was not a member of the psychology department. After a few minutes of failed attempts to gain access to the secretary's office, he finally glanced in my direction in a puzzled manner. I informed him that I was writing a book on "Aging". I told him of some of the discoveries which I had learned in my research. Of special interest I stated, was the notion that after age 60 there was a decrement in cognition and memory. I informed Professor Henry of some discoveries pertaining to aging and mentioned during the senior years one had to expect changes in previously accomplished abilities. Professor Henry mentioned he did not agree with the information on aging and expressed that he was well into his 60's and still quite adept at intellectual pursuits. He proudly stated that he had a better memory than younger colleagues in his department. In the next breath, he asked where the secretary was so that he could gain access to the office; he wanted to obtain his mail. It was his impression that she must have changed the lock on the door because his key would not open it. I informed this bewildered professor the secretary was probably at lunch. I further mentioned to Professor Henry that he was in the wrong department and he should go down the hallway to his own department and try his key on the secretary's door. Professor Henry at first seemed a little bewildered by the incident and then went off hastily in the direction of his department not showing any noticeable sign of embarrassment. In his mind, he was likely elated because he would finally get access to his mail. In this example, Professor Henry had made an error in recognizing that he was not only in the wrong department but also that he had failed to recognize the reason for his inability to open the door lock. He had assumed the secretary had changed the lock. This is a good example of loss of crystallized and fluid memory ability in a post 65 year old academic.

During their senior years, people have difficulty recognizing changes in their environment. This implies that seniors may be aware changes have occurred in their workplace or home but aren't immediately able to recognize the degree of change which has taken place. Psychologists refer to small perceptual changes as "just noticeable differences". As the senior person ages, he or she may not be aware of the minor changes which occur in sensory information they are evaluating. Consequently, they must be capable of making quick cognitive shifts by using their fluid intellectual ability. One must be capable of quickly making comparisons and decisions as they encode information. It is not a question of whether seniors have memory impairments but whether they have the ability to recognize these impairments. When this happens, seniors require strategies to cope.

It is one thing to forget the location of one's car in a parking lot, but a greater problem when a professor forgets that he has taught a lecture and repeats the same lecture the next day. It is a problem of greater magnitude when a professor gives a test in one semester only to re-administer the same test in the next semester because of memory deficiency. It is of greatest concern when a professor looses his way to the university because of a memory related disorder such as Alzheimer disease.

My clinical practise has allowed me to work with seniors in Inpatient Facilities. These people were referred for psychological evaluation because of intellectual and memory decrements. Some of these patients had been requested to undergo assessment because they were getting lost when they went for a walk in their neighbourhood. Others were posing safety concerns by forgetting to turn off stove burners or putting their milk in the cupboard rather than in the refrigerator. In general, an evaluation of these seniors showed gross impairment in cognitive and memory abilities. These extreme examples of aging decrements allow the reader to recognize the ramifications of aging and its impact on one's health and welfare. Not only is the senior, the victim of the aging process but the relatives and friends also become involved because they have to ensure their loved one is not at physical risk.

It is a fact of life that aging causes a decline in memory. Unless one has a serious decrement in memory however, it does not become of paramount importance. Most seniors can learn effective ways of coping with small changes in memory. Many seniors use techniques including writing pads to compile personal notes to remind themselves of important tasks or events. This technique assists the person to contend with failing memory. Furthermore, there has been some data to show that memory impairment might be traced to a genetic marker. The research of Ruth Frikke-Schmidt and her colleagues has shown a genetic basis (ie. APOE e4allele) to Alzheimer's disease. Furthermore, research by Mary Tierney and her colleagues has shown that neuropsychological testing has proven of paramount importance in providing substantial data that assists in distinguishing "normal aging from dementia" (ie. vascular and other types including Alzheimer's disease). Researchers have noted that seniors who are aware of their increased probability for dementia or Alzheimer's can make decisions to undergo detailed neuropsychological assessment. Having this insight can provide some assistance in planning for oneself in the event a cognitive impairment occurs.

Memory Improvement with Drug Therapy:
There has been some debate on the use of drugs to enhance memory function. As early as the 1970's psychologist James McConnell evaluated memory in lower organisms known as planaria. These small flat worm species were taught through conditioning experiments to perform recall tasks. Later on, the original planaria who had mastered the task were ground up and fed to other planaria. The planaria who had been fed the "ground up planaria learners" did much better on the same memory task at a later date. The point here is that one does not need to practise cannibalism of smarter individuals to enhance memory. The message which James McConnell was implying from his research would indicate the basis of memory is stored in chemical messengers found in DNA.

Through the use of DNA chemicals one might enhance their cognitive processing ability.

Since the onset of McConnell's experimentation, research has evaluated the influence of drugs on memory. Pharmaceutical companies and the health food industry seem to be the purveyors of these claims because they have much to gain from the sale of vitamins, minerals and other complex herbal substances which enhance memory and increase intelligence. Health food stores have made claims in their promotions that taking additives for example DNA complex will enhance brain activity. Others including Benno Roosendaal and his colleague have noted the use of glucocorticoids either prior to or immediately after a learning experience enhances the long term storage of the newly acquired memory. Apparently, this is consistent with research which found memories learned under stressful conditions (ie. post-traumatic incidents) were easily remembered and later haunted their victims over lengthy periods of time. There is also evidence which notes that people under continued stress have major difficulty with their memory because the glucocorticoids may have a significant impact on the amygdala (fear/anxiety centre) and/or the hippocampus (memory centre). The hippocampus and the amygdala are directly involved with the storage of information. Since the hippocampus appears to facilitate the encoding of memories, any negative stimulus which interferes with retention will have an impact on either the storage or retrieval process. Some researchers have investigated remembering in males and females and found unique gender differences. Ostensibly, biochemical levels of estrogen, decline in women during menopause. Estrogen loss has an apparent impact on memory retention in women. Apparently after menopause, women become more forgetful. Hormone replacement therapy however has been found to be of assistance in improving memory deficiency for menopausal women.

One begins to realize there are certain strategies a senior person can utilize to elevate memory potential. It is possible to teach seniors cognitive strategies which will enhance brain potential. The cerebral cortex has some plasticity to it and there is growing information to suggest that the brain has the ability to regenerate through the growth of new cells. New strategies must be advanced to assist seniors in learning the skills which can increase brain potential. Many of these strategies would encourage seniors to engage in cognitive skills which force their brain to learn new information.

There are many factors including biological and environmental which can decrease memory. Research has shown that one must have a sound sensory system to uptake information and a hippocampus capable of encoding and storing memories. If the hippocampus is affected by too many environmental or personal stressors, then the individual will show inability to process information readily. Research by Louise Hawkley and her colleagues found deleterious effects on organ systems subjected to stressors. If one experiences stress frequently or the magnitude of the stressor exceeds one's capacity for adaptability, then exhaustion or death could occur to the organism. The lifestyle choices of the senior should limit exposure to stress. Seniors who are healthy and have responsive organ systems will be more adaptive. Whether this means leaving stressful situations which are beyond one's control, the degree of one's resiliency will determine the impact of stress on the biological system.

Summary and Conclusions:

It would seem that the best way to ensure sound cognitive functioning during the senior years is through diet, exercise and daily activities. Enrolling in ongoing educational and brain activity programs would also be of some benefit to seniors because these activities force thinking, planning and strategizing and engage the frontal lobes in novel challenges.

CHAPTER THREE

SUCCESSFUL AGING

Rule #4: Successful aging requires self-acceptance.

What does it mean to age successfully? In my interaction with people over the age of 50, I have obtained many opinions. A common theme which flows from their ideas is the notion that one should have a daily plan and live each day to the fullest. Having achieved the age of 50, one shouldn't consider themselves old, but merely having had more experience with life. For many, it will be a time to reflect on their accomplishments and provide some goals for the next fifty years of their life.

Some researchers have evaluated seniors and found varied results on successful aging. For example, Carol Gold and her colleagues evaluated men and women; they found women had a more positive outlook regarding life than men. A central theme which emerged indicated women's positive attitude was a result of their ongoing social interactions with other women. Men however, tended to be more isolated and detached from social circles; they did not experience the same outlook on life.

According to some, successful aging occurs when an individual obtains maximum happiness and satisfaction. For successful aging to occur, seniors must maximize their goals in life but at the same time enjoy every situation they experience. Rather then proceeding through life with the view that every event will be onerous, seniors need to re-focus their beliefs and embellish their accomplishments. Aging successfully is the ability to adjust positively to the everyday demands one experiences in their lives. An interesting finding by Gary Reker and his colleagues has shown that the more satisfied seniors were with life, the more anxiety they had regarding death. This is understandable because happy and healthy people don't look forward to dying. They view their lives with optimism and look forward to each day because it brings a sense of fulfilment.

One must have the ability to meet the challenges which arise in everyday life; to react positively to these events and accept them with ease. A study by Noralou Roos and Leslie Roos showed that approximately 20% of a selected population between the ages of 65 to 84 was judged to have achieved successful aging as noted from their health records. When gender was evaluated, the data showed that women were healthier and had higher life satisfaction than men. Of the variables evaluated, physical health appeared to be the most important factor that promoted successful aging. This is consistent with the views of many practitioners including Jo-Anne Clarke, a geriatrician. She believes that successful aging is the ability to live disability free. By having sound physical ability one can engage in many diverse activities.

Statistics Canada would agree the incidence of

disease, escalates after the age of 60. However, one does not have to assume just because they are over the age of 60, they will succumb to some disease process. On a daily basis, I encounter many people at the gym who are well over the age of 60 they appear to be in fine physical health. Exercise programs assist them in retaining their youthful vigour.

Bradley Fisher found from his interviews with older seniors that successful aging seemed to be dependent on satisfaction experienced in life. Many seniors evaluate their accomplishments as a function of how they have lived their lives. To some, satisfaction is a result of productive career, health, spousal selection and personal attitude. A set of collective experiences become personally important to seniors. This perception is upheld by many as noted from the work of Gale Gray and her colleagues who found that one's ability to interact with others assisted a person in coping with life. Seniors who had received emotional support from friends and family were more satisfied with their life.

According to some authors, there are a number of factors which lead to successful aging. Erdman Palmore has discovered successful aging includes survival until age 75, healthy physical ability, and an elevated sense of happiness. People who were more physically active were happier than those who could not engage in physical activities. Others, including Carol Ryff have noted that self-acceptance, autonomy, purpose in life, personal growth, positive relations with others and environmental mastery lead to successful aging.

George Vaillant, a medical practitioner at the Brigham and Women's Hospital in Boston, and a professor at Harvard Medical School, believes one's ancestral longevity seems to be associated with well-being in later life. Seniors who have viable genes, have a better chance for increased longevity. Vaillant's longitudinal research further showed the most important factors in aging successfully included a stable marriage, adaptation to everyday problems/strife, moderate use of alcohol, avoidance of tobacco, reasonable level of education, regular exercise and the maintenance of one's weight. Apparently seniors who practised these styles of living were better able to adjust to life. He referred to these seniors as "successful agers". These seniors engaged in activities which lead to a positive lifestyle.

From my research, I have found specific factors contribute to a successful lifestyle. The factors listed below have emerged as important variables needed for successful aging:

1) Ancestral Longevity:
Lineage, allows one to evaluate their genetic pool. It is difficult to foresee the length of time one will live. A good place to start would be to investigate the length of time one's ancestors have lived. Grandparents and parents on maternal and paternal sides are an ideal starting point. If both sets of ancestors have lived into their eighties the chance of reaching this age is highly probable. The senior must remember that telomeres are at the basis of longevity. Some people have been favoured by durable long strand telomeres which make their cells more resilient to the aging process. Telomerase the enzyme which prevents the telomeres from deterioration is also of importance.

2) Exercise:

Seniors can benefit from regular ongoing exercise. I have been a consumer of this motto for some 35 years and can attest to the importance of good health. My daily exercise program includes stretching, light weights, cardiovascular activities (ie. treadmill, cross trainer, elliptical, jogging, or bicycling). Exercise provides many benefits including conditioning the heart and lungs. I have known many patients who have experienced myocardial infarcts. Luckily, they survived because the attending physician in the Emergency Room, quickly administered streptokinase upon admittance to the hospital. Later diagnosis of those who had active exercise programs showed less arterial blockage and showed quicker recovery than sedentary patients who had not exercised. Medical specialists who completed post-operative evaluation remarked that regular exercise, having a proper diet, and not using tobacco products, had increased one's rate of survival. According to the medical specialists, patients with similar medical conditions who had harmful habits (ie. smoking, heavy alcohol consumption) had died of complications following their myocardial infarcts.

Many seniors have the physical capability of involving themselves in exercise programs. Some readily pursue physical activity, and some pursue these on an irregular basis; whereas others never become involved in exercise programs. The advantages of exercise programs are numerous, but some people never become involved in physical activity. It is a known fact that seniors who become involved in exercise later in life also show beneficial effects. It is important for the senior, to discover an activity they enjoy and get started. Exercise will improve one's physical health and make longevity a reality.

3) Stability of Emotions:
Many seniors seek emotional stability in later years. Stability is not only good for physical health but also for mental health. Research supports the notion that people who are emotionally healthy have better social relationships, marriages and physical health in later years. To achieve emotional health, one must have had a stable period of growth during formative development. In David Abrahamsen's book, "The Road to Emotional Maturity", an exploration of factors leading to later emotional maturity were explored. Much like the message posited by early psychodynamic therapists, the author infers healthy emotional patterns of behaviour preclude sound emotional adjustment in later stages of life. The child attempts to master each stage of development, then later pushes forward to undertake mastery of their life.

At the basis of emotional health, is the need to accept oneself. Self-acceptance allows one to establish beneficial interpersonal relationship with others. One must have good emotional stability, high self-esteem and positive self-worth before moving toward the acceptance of others. People who have had good stability throughout their lives reach their senior years with an acceptance of self which allows them to love and appreciate others. Within each person is an inner self which yearns for acceptance.

During childhood, one seeks affection, approval and bonding with parents. The positive verbal feedback the child receives from parents provides reassurance and emotional support. Later, non-verbal gestures are sufficient to provide emotional support. Eventually, children learn a sense of self-acceptance. In their interactions with parents, children like to imitate. By imitating verbal and physical behaviour, social rules are learned; reinforcement is given when the child expresses prosocial behaviour. Many studies have documented the importance of learning through imitation and modelling. In the classic study by Albert Bandura, children imitated the actions of adult role models and identified with them so they would receive acceptance. Children are motivated to exhibit acceptable behaviour; they will go to great lengths to achieve this. Identification with the parent provides children with an avenue leading to acceptance. Positive bonding is at the basis of these supportive relationships.

The power of biological attachment is established early in life. The research findings of Konrad Lorenz with lower organisms showed that innate behaviour patterns are "imprinted" in the young. This fixed action pattern of "imprinting" appears to enhance the survival of the species. Humans also engage in a type of "imprinting" but unlike the avian species, humans use verbal and non-verbal gestures to strengthen the bonds between child and adult. By doing so allows the human species to not only survive but also to learn adaptive social skills.

Mastering self-acceptance can be immediate for some and for others can only be learned over a life time. The key element behind self-acceptance may be genetically programmed in our emotional behaviour and emerges as a facet of our personality. Many who reach their senior years but are in a state of flux because of lack of mastery of self-acceptance, have a tougher time adjusting to the process of aging. In his writings, Erik Erikson formulated the concept of self-acceptance. In the initial developmental stages, the child attempts to establish trust, autonomy and initiative. Parents are instrumental in the provision of emotional support to their children during these three stages. Some parents hinder emotional growth through poor parenting practices which may cause the child to not develop. For example, if the parent only provides negative feedback, this can hinder the child's emotional development and thereby lead to an inability for self-acceptance and self-love.

By the fourth stage of growth known as industry/inferiority which takes place from about age 6 to 12, the child attempts to become competent and adjusted to the world around him/her. The child's confidence in finding acceptance from peers or adult role models will allow for successful social integration. Being reinforced by teachers and important others, allows the child to perceive others as accepting and caring individuals. The success a child receives from their interaction with others ultimately allows him or her to go forth and become engaged in activities. A child who becomes fixated at this stage will have trouble coping with social/emotional challenges. This could lead to later problems in adulthood. The child who falters at this stage could conceivably question their competence at fitting in with others. Ultimately, the child evaluates himself or herself as having less ability in mastering the world. Individuals who have had repeated failure with adjustment to life's expectation will develop an attitude of non-accomplishment. This could lead to less esteem and to an inferiority complex. They could experience a sense of despair in their later years because their emotional development has faltered.

According to Erikson, those who "fixate" at an early stage do not function well in relationships. These people are unable to achieve a sense of worth. From adolescence to senescence a person goes through four further stages of growth. Each of these stages must be handled competently to ensure attainment of identity, intimacy, generativity and integrity. Faltering at these stages can lead to role confusion, isolation, self-absorption and despair. For seniors who have not mastered each stage, they risk the chance of not becoming "self-actualized" to coin Abraham Maslow's terminology.

In my role as a psychologist, I have encountered many people with personal and emotional difficulties. A common denominator which tends to emerge in these individuals is lack of personal acceptance. Not only do these people have the inability to accept themselves, but they believe that others are not accepting of them. People have a deeply rooted need to be loved and many struggle to have this need fulfilled. Seniors need to be loved and accepted but they must also have the emotional disposition which will encourage others to love them. It is difficult to expect to be loved and accepted if one is egocentric and demanding. To be successful at aging, it is important for seniors to have a sense of personal well-being.

4) Autonomy:

Many people strive for their individuality. The ability to function without the interference from others is an important attribute. As one ages, there is less of a need to be dependent on others, unless of course, one is physically, emotionally or mentally challenged. With adequate income provided by one's retirement savings, the senior can obtain independence. Becoming independent in society is an important part of the transition to successful aging. One does not have to conform to the pressures and expectations of others. Those with self-mastery look toward successful aging as a stage in which they can break away from the status quo. Success can be measured by ones ability to become disengaged from the workforce. One can commence travel plans and move to a new locale to begin their retirement. Seniors must learn to exist without the assistance of others.

Some seniors seek independence in order to achieve positive growth. Others become mired in their habits and only find solace in a setting in which they have become accustomed. Some people have a personality and lifestyle orientation that cause them to seek continuity of sameness. They don't want to become disengaged from habits and/or acquaintances. These people are happy and show positive growth not from change but with continuity of habit. For these seniors, a change in lifestyle could cause undue anxiety. Some seniors have order infused in their daily lives, as they interact with family and friends. Their personal nature encourages them to engage in daily rituals and routine. Conversely, some seniors do not like routine. They prefer novel situations so they can feel stimulated and alive. Personality often determines one's choice of lifestyle.

5) Purpose in Life:
After the age of 50, seniors begin to question the meaning of existence? Erik Erikson believed ones purpose in life was a function of their perception of what is satisfying. Some seniors evaluate their lives in terms of their success at raising a family, others by their productivity in the workforce, and some by their fulfilment of personal goals. The senior who pursues objectives, recognizes the importance of goals. They perceive a need to fulfil their dreams. By doing so, they

obtain happiness and satisfaction from their lives. Seniors who achieve their goals seem happiest with their existence. By fulfilling their life's dreams, they obtain a degree of satisfaction. Conversely, seniors who have had goals but never attempted to fulfil these because they had a fear of failure become discontent with their lives. Successful aging appears to be dependent on fulfilling expectations. In his book, "The 7 Habits of Highly Effective People", Richard Covey indicates that people should attempt to evaluate their lives with the end of their life in mind. They should think about what they would like to have accomplished in their life and work backwards attempting to envision what they would have to do to achieve these goals. By prioritizing one's life, assists with a plan for self-actualization.

6) Personal Growth:
One must pursue personal growth in order to age successfully. I have taught full time in a university setting for some 32 years. During this time, students have often asked "when will I be able to stop studying". I explain to them, they can never discontinue their studies. Learning maintains their brain in a state of optimal arousal and allows one to cognitively flourish. Successful aging is like learning, it is a process that cannot be discontinued. One must never stop learning if they want to age successfully. Research on aging indicates that intelligence peaks during the mid 20's and levels off at middle age. Once learning is discontinued, there is a quicker decline in cognitive and intellectual ability. To age quickly would require that one discontinue activities which engage cortical processing.

The data on aging indicates that by the time one is approximately 60 years of age there will be a decrease in the number of neurons in the brain. The research on cortical activity shows that seniors who continue to challenge themselves daily by engaging in activities which exercise their mind, age at a slower rate. In a recent Carp Health e-Bulletin, I read an article by David Cravit entitled, "Did You Have Your Brain Workout Today". In the article prepared by www.50Plus.com, Bernard Croisile, affiliated with the Neuropsychology Department at the Neurological Hospital in Lyon France was interviewed about his cognitive training program, "Happy Neuron". The good doctor indicated the cognitive training program was designed to improve brain performance through the use of cognitive exercises, which extended over a 45 minute period, 2-3 times a week. The program utilized games to improve memory, attention, language, executive function (decision making) and visual-spatial relationships. This allowed for communication across the left and right hemispheres. According to Dr. Croisile, cortical connections within the brain are diminished by the aging process. Over time, the brain becomes impaired in its ability to function. Cognitive training exercises create new cortical connections. From the research done on brain exercise programs, it would appear that seniors should undertake a cognitive program which stimulates multi-levels of the brain. Through this type of activity, one can engage the cerebral cortex thereby enhancing cognitive processing.

Seniors do not have to accept aging as some process which is synonymous with dying. Although older people will eventually die, one does not have to cease all activities in preparation for their death. Seniors can continue to learn and engage in life every day regardless of age or circumstance. Recently, I was on my way to the classroom to give a lecture. A senior lady, approximately 70 years of age stopped me; she wanted to know the way to the English department. Apparently she had contemplated returning to university as a mature student. By enrolling in an English program, she would be challenging her brain. Seniors should never let age dictate the direction of their lives. Physical and cortical activity can engage sensory, motor and cortical neurons.

7). Positive Relationships with Others:

Before you can love and appreciate relationships with others, you must love yourself. One must appreciate themselves as worthwhile. Erik Erikson's developmental model is an important reference point for emotional health. I often tell students in first year psychology that emotional health is not entirely genetic but learned as one proceeds through life's stages. Problems in life can interfere with productive emotional growth. When problematic issues arise, one must learn to cope with conflict or risk future emotional issues. A buzz word of the early 2000's was the terminology "dysfunctional behaviour". Dysfunctional behaviour according to experts arose from early problematic issues during one's life. The message was clear that dysfunction was caused by negative experiences which occurred during one's formative development. Many have used the term to describe trauma caused by problematic interpersonal relationships. Once afflicted by problems, the victim is unable to move forward with their life. Early developmental problems cause emotional dilemma. Without a sense of self, the "dysfunctional victim" is thwarted from achieving an emotionally healthy status. Rather than attempting to establish a sense of emotional competency, the dysfunctional person becomes dependent on others. Those who are "dysfunctional" have difficulty working toward personal objectives on their own; they believe others should assist and provide for their emotional needs. This only leads to dependency and does not allow the person to become self-sufficient.

Relationships with others have a marked effect on emotional and mental health. It appears from George Vaillant's research that married people were more successful at aging than divorced people. Other researchers have also noted that married men have better mental health than married women but conversely unmarried men have poorer mental health than unmarried women. Some have proposed that married women are in a more demanding role and this places them at greater psychological risk for emotional disorders than married men. As men age, they tend to become more reliant on their spouses for emotional support but in turn cannot provide the same emotional support to their spouses. Cecile Quirouette and Dolores Gold believe the added responsibility in some relationships especially where men are required to be responsible for their wives financial well-being, predisposes them to show less emotional support to their wives. Married women conversely look toward children and friends for emotional support. When this is not available, married women become more depressed and less content with their lifestyle. Future research will likely affirm that people who interact positively with others as they age, will have a greater propensity to exhibit healthier life attitudes than those who are detached and lonely.

Human beings are social organisms and need others with whom they can interact. It is beneficial for people to have healthy and stable relationships. Spouses who are emotionally supportive are more willing to give and receive emotional support and provide positive feedback in relationships. This allows for a constant exchange of verbal and non-verbal information, thus creating better bonding in the relationship.

8) Mastering the Environment:
How does one master their environment? Erik Erikson advocated that mastery of one's environment can only be obtained by effort. Without effort their can be no gain. One must have the courage to attempt a task and the courage to accept defeat. There will always be hurdles in life. In his writing, Kurt Lewin believed that each of us is faced with obstacles in our life; challenging these can lead to some personal insight and mastery of our destiny. The senior person faces many challenges throughout their lives. Those who have cleared hurdles and coped with challenges can look back on their achievements and realize a sense of accomplishment. Those who have successfully mastered their achievements have an imminent satisfaction with their life. Irvine Yalom believed that one who has experienced failure, but forges ahead with their life, achieves the greatest understanding of their existence. One must acknowledge that human nature has its frailties and these sometimes get in the way of achieving goals. To fail at something means that one must accept defeat but put forth effort in an attempt to solidify their goals.

As one ages, there is a need to be content with life. The senior must view aging as a time of change. Even with declining physical health, a sense of meaning can be achieved. Goal fulfilment can be evaluated as one recalls their life's experiences. Pleasant memories can assist the senior in remembering positive experiences. Those who have a positive view of life experience more satisfaction than those who only focus on the negative aspects of life.

9) Physical Health and Diet:

Many studies have concluded that restricting one's diet will prolong life. Research with lower organisms (ie. rats, mice) and higher organisms (ie. humans) has shown that limiting daily caloric intake will extend life. The notion that tends to surface in the literature would concur that "thin is in" and "stout is out". The early research of Alexander Leaf and John Launois with European and South American centenarians and more recent research on Asian dietary intake, indicates that people who consume fewer calories on a daily basis and restrict their diets to fish, lean meat, and vegetables, live longer lives. People with greater daily caloric intake and a higher intake of carbohydrates and polysaturated fat diets, face debilitating diseases in their senior years; they do not live as long.

Other contributing factors to longevity include removing free radicals from the body. As oxygen is consumed by cells, free radicals emerge as by-products, which can attack and destroy cells. According to James Duke, the aging person can do much to avoid the build-up of these oxygen free radicals. The daily use of antioxidants and vitamins found in fruit and vegetables, remove free radicals thereby thwarting the effects of aging.

CHAPTER FOUR

PHYSICAL HEALTH

Rule #5: Exercising leads to a reduction in the aging process.

There are many ways of increasing longevity in the senior years. One proven way has been through the implementation of an exercise program. Some research has shown that regular exercise increases telomere durability. Comparison of seniors who exercise regularly, show they have the physiological ability of people who are 10 years younger. The adage of "healthy body-healthy mind" seems to prevail because seniors who are actively engaged in exercise programs not only live longer but gain more satisfaction out of life. People who are in better shape physically, are more mobile and become more active in daily activities. They have the ability to cope with stress. These people enjoy life to the fullest because of their physiological stamina.

The Behaviour Risk Factor Surveillance System showed that between 1994 and 1996, approximately 30% of adults 55 to 74 years of age were physically inactive. This percentage increased to 46% for seniors over the age of 75 years. These statistics are not surprising since many seniors have the belief that physical activity will not be of benefit or perhaps harmful to them especially when they reach age 70. Many people are neophobic and afraid to engage in novel tasks especially exercise. They have the impression that changing their sedentary style to one which is more physically engaging will not benefit them. This underlying scepticism seems to prevail in their attitude. Seniors need to be encouraged by friends or family members to commence physical activity. In time, seniors will begin to realize that exercise is of some benefit. Once they develop a routine and begin to follow a daily schedule, they will begin to appreciate the impact on lifestyle.

Exercise:
From ongoing research with seniors, it appears that exercise is beneficial to the elderly because this assists them in maintaining sensory-motor integrity. Data collected in one of my research projects showed that physical activity promoted emotional health and decreased depressive mood in seniors. Russell Pate and his associates have shown that physical ailments including cardiovascular diseases can be controlled by increased physical activity especially during senescence. Christian Werner and his colleagues have found that physical activity regulates telomere deterioration in older people. This can in turn protect them from stress-induced vascular deterioration. Researchers have also noted that elderly athletes who had a long-term history of continuous exercise showed elevated leucocyte telomerase and conservation of telomere length in their cells. This would imply that seniors who

engage in regular exercise programs improve molecular activity of the protein in the telomeres thereby providing themselves with a built in anti-aging formula. Exercise influences the health of the cells and the organ systems. Those who exercise, age more slowly than their counterparts who do not involve themselves in regular activity.

Today, there is an increased demand on individuals to exercise. This message has influenced a large segment of the population to become aware of the importance of exercise on sensory-motor systems and the brain. Exercise can enhance telomere durability and delay the aging process. Many people over the age of 50 are now showing increased interest in exercise and spend a number of hours each week in pursuit of physical conditioning. It is imperative that seniors receive a complete medical examination prior to undertaking vigorous activity. Exercise could place them at health risk if they are not in good physical health. By knowing one's limitations prior to beginning an exercise program could prevent serious physical consequences.

Realistically speaking, not all seniors are ready to initiate physical exercise programs. They have to investigate the avenues available prior to embarking on this path. Programs including walking, cycling, swimming, jogging, weight lifting, dancing, skiing or bowling can provide a point of entry for seniors. Other alternatives including Tai Chi or Yoga may appeal to those who prefer a solitary and less physically demanding pursuit. Some seniors have an abhorrent distaste for physical exercise because it leaves them tired and exhausted. Research has shown that exercise initiated before the muscle tissue is properly "warmed" may cause injury. It is advantageous for seniors to receive a physical evaluation prior to commencing a program. One can seek the guidance of a qualified trainer to provide an exercise program geared to one's level of fitness. The trainer can design a program which provides the senior with a series of exercises. Prior to exercising the importance of warm-ups can be emphasized. At the completion of the program, a series of warm-down exercises are undertaken to reduce the strain on the muscle groups. An exercise program which is inculcated into a daily program should not leave the senior exhausted.

One's temperament or more specifically personality can also have some impact on exercise. For example, an earlier study by Valliant in 1979 showed specific personality traits were associated with injury predisposition. This study showed that joggers who became injured while exercising were "rigid and more compulsive" than a non-injured group of joggers. A rigid personality style coupled with a compulsive nature leads to a higher degree of injury. This generally occurs because rigid people tend to be more tense and unable to vary the type of training regime in which they are engaged. It would appear that some joggers have internal beliefs which interfere with their approach toward exercise. It is important for those who haven't developed an exercise regime before the age of 50, to discuss the advent of a suitable program with a qualified trainer. This will reduce the chance of injury. Second, it is important that seniors decide upon a physical activity or exercise program of interest to themselves. This will enhance their motivation to continue with the activity. The type of program one decides upon should complement lifestyle and accessibility to equipment. A behavioral evaluation could also assist in examining underlying factors including personality and temperament which drive the senior toward a sport.

Last, it is imperative that seniors hire a trainer with expertise regarding the physical activity chosen. A trainer will not only have knowledge of the proper techniques to be used in the program but will also have knowledge of diet which could assist the senior in preparing for the training regime. Proper diet and supplements will allow one to maintain optimal performance and not experience exhaustion or injury.

Prior to undertaking an exercise program, it is imperative that one has the proper mental conditioning required for the activity. One must have the interest toward the exercise program/sport and second they must have the proper conditioning to engage in that sport. Third, they must have some knowledge of the method used in the pursuit of the activity. For example, the swimmer must know the type of strokes needed to traverse the pool; while the jogger must be aware of the proper shoes required for the terrain they are about to run; and the weight lifter some familiarity with the weights and types of exercises needed to condition certain muscle groups. The person who is about to undertake exercise, must be provided with the skills needed to engage in the activity. This knowledge can be gained through the auspices of a trainer who has undertaken specialty courses. The trainer will provide the novice exerciser with the expertise needed to undertake physical conditioning. Once a skill is learned, the senior will require practise to ensure retention of the activity.

After commencing an exercise program not all seniors will continue with this activity. Some will become bored with the program. Humans seek change in their daily routine, otherwise the activity becomes monotonous. Boredom is defined as a lack of motivation resulting from disinterest in the activity. It is important for the exerciser to think of ways of enhancing their active involvement in a program. For example, joggers may become bored with running a track and seek to enlarge their training regime. One way of doing this is by including fartlek training. By varying the speed of the run allows them to combat boredom. By increasing their aerobic cardiovascular and pulmonary activity they may experience the "high" created by the release of endorphins (beta enkephalins) into the brain. This generally requires about 30 minutes of intense activity before these natural brain opiates are released. Jogging can become addictive because of the endorphin release. A colleague once asked if I had ever seen a "happy jogger". I responded that joggers never seem happy during their run, however after it is over they experience an altered state because of the release of endorphins in the brain. Having personally jogged for years, and trained rigorously to compete in marathons, I have been able to attest to the state of exhilaration experienced from the endorphin release. The "runners high" created by the brain's own opiate substance, creates an altered state of mood. Most joggers will continue with their running program because they seek; 1) physical conditioning and 2) the euphoric state experienced after the run is over.

When one begins an activity program, the end result must be evaluated. After strenuous involvement in a physical activity, a biochemical evaluation shows a significant change in the LDL/HDL cholesterol ratio. Improved cardiovascular, respiratory and increased muscle strength leads to the combined extrinsic (physical benefits from the exercise) and the intrinsic (internalized feelings from accomplishment) gained from the activity. Many exercises have their rewards; which include the biochemical effects as well as the accomplishment experienced from completion of the activity. Other benefits include improved physiological stamina, good health, and the camaraderie of being with others.

Research by Danielle Laurin and her associates have found that men and women over the age of 65 who exercised regularly showed lower risks of cognitive impairment, Alzheimer disease, and dementia. Physical activity causes stimulation of the parietal lobes (sensory brain) which in turn activates the pre-motor and motor areas of the frontal lobes. This stimulation causes the frontal brain to become engaged and releases a cortical response. The exerciser becomes more active cerebrally as sensory and motor information course through the brain and lower body. Activation of the central nervous system creates a holistic brain-body interaction. The end result is the engagement of the individual's brain, spinal chord and organ systems.

There are many advantages of exercising. By the time one reaches age 50, the body is beginning to show the effects of physiological deterioration. Cognitively and physically one's body is on the decline. Thinking, memory, intelligence, sensory and motor movement begin to show deterioration. Many seniors seek ways of offsetting this process. Those who engage in physical activity, indicate that exercise creates physical duress and bouts of pain. However they learn to adjust their level of output during the activity. Some seniors can't jog or use a treadmill because of joint pain, but they pursue other activities including stretching or swimming. On days when they feel more vigorous they lift weights. People have informed me the best way to approach exercise is by "listening to their body". They learn to adjust their exercise programs to their physical and motivational needs. Also, on days when they don't feel like undertaking vigorous exercise, less active forms of exercise including stretching, yoga or tai chi can be undertaken.

Motivation has always been one of the major concerns of seniors who undertake exercise programs. Many reasons given for engaging in exercise programs include; increased energy, stamina, muscle strength and the ability to undertake activities to enhance one's vitality. There is growing evidence to suggest that physically fit seniors exhibit less dramatic changes in thinking during the aging process. One has heard the adage "health body and healthy mind". Ostensibly physical activity encourages sensory-motor activity through the parietal-frontal lobe connection. The physically active senior has more than just their sensory and motor neurons activated. In the process of exercising, one exerts frontal brain activity. The planning and execution of activities in turn increases cognitive processing. Physically fit seniors describe themselves as being happier and more content with their lifestyle. By exercising frequently, the senior becomes more energetic and is capable of involvement in a wider range of other life activities.

Information shows that cognitive processing (ie. thinking, reasoning and decision making) appears to be enhanced by the advent of sport. Research by Wojtek Chodzko-Zajko and his colleagues have examined the association between physical fitness and performance on complex thinking tasks. Specific tasks which included motor movement (ie. walking, jogging) greatly enhanced memory; it was not only improved by undertaking motor tasks, but also seniors gained from the physiological benefit of the exercise. A comparison of seniors with younger and middle age persons, showed similar ability in memory tasks; seniors who exercised regularly had improved memory. Wojtek Chodzko-Zajko and his colleagues have proposed that seniors who were less fit and less cognitively active showed the most improvement in memory following participation in fitness programs. I have investigated the effects of exercise on physiology and mood in seniors between the age of 50 and 80 years. The results of the study showed that seniors who were involved in fitness programs, had more elevated mood (ie. lower depression scores), less fear and higher self-esteem than their counterparts not involved in physical activity programs. During the aging process, one undergoes a number of physical changes in cognition, emotion and personality. Seniors seek ways to increase physical and emotional health. Bernice Neugarten has noted that people have to be adaptable during their senescent years. Seniors who have a positive attitude can face novel challenges and engage in adaptive lifestyles which in turn will encourage emotional growth. Retired people have more time to engage in a healthy lifestyle. This promotes physical, emotional and mental health. According to Bernice Neugarten, the senior person who seeks out new challenges can become socially and physically engaged and more content with their lifestyle.

Rule #6: Eating natural food promotes better aging.

DIET:
Hunger, thirst and sexuality are three primary emotions which motivate the human species. The first two are necessary for life, without them one would perish. Dieticians have

advocated for healthy lifestyles. They inform us consumption of the essential food groups are necessary for good health. Scientists have investigated the biochemical properties of food groups and their effect on health. This has led to greater awareness of substances necessary for physical well-being. In North America alone, approximately 4.5 billion dollars are spent on dietary supplements every year because many people believe that food alone does not have all the nutrient requirements necessary for one's physiological needs. The aging population is continually looking for an elixir to enhance their health. The supplements they use have some of the nutrients which assist in their drive for longevity.

People strive to look and feel better and prolong their physical health. This ideology appears to be at the basis of the search for the "elixirs" which will prevent ill health. Disease lingers covertly within our bodies waiting to take hold and destroy us. To thwart these, one must build a healthy and sustainable immune system. As one ages, the cells within the immune system begin to wear down, and age related diseases have a way of creeping into the body. It is imperative that people search for ways of enhancing the immune system through the use of natural products. For example, one of the main components of garlic is a substance known as allicin. This substance wards off viruses and bacteria. Other natural products including Co-enzyme Q10 and Echinacea can also be used to build a stronger and efficient immune system.

Natural substances are abundant as phytochemicals in a variety of fruits and vegetables. The have chemically rich properties to assist in maintaining health and vitality. Many natural food products are also loaded with vitamins and minerals. These are necessary for longevity and are a panacea for increased well-being. Natural substances however have to be investigated thoroughly prior to being included in one's diet. For example, Ginkgo Biloba first appeared in the market place about a decade ago. It was described as a substance which would restore memory in seniors experiencing cognitive deterioration. Millions of dollars were spent by the populace in self-administration of this herbal medicine in anticipation that one's "memory centre" would be spared from the ravages of old age. Recent research by Steven Dekosky and his colleagues, found that after a 6 year longitudinal study, Ginkgo Biloba was deemed as having no significant effect on the improvement of memory. People who self-prescribed this herbal drug showed no significant gains in memory. This example provides some evidence that pharmaceutical companies undertake research because of their need to create a market and profit from the sale of drugs. In their attempt to restore memory function in those afflicted by cognitive decline, many avenues are used to discover a "wonder drug".

Al Sears has undertaken some promising research at his Health and Wellness Centre in Royal Palm Beach in Florida. He has discovered that specific chemicals can decrease and possibly even reverse the aging process. Administration of a chemical referred to as TA-65 replete with a component known as astragalus can reduce the aging process. TA-65 apparently triggers a gene in cells to produce telomerase. As mentioned earlier, telomerase hinders the deterioration of the telomeres as the cells divide. This is turn increases the durability of the cell and decreases the aging process. Furthermore, Al Sears has advocated that to reduce the aging process, one has to control the level of homocysteine in cells. Apparently homocysteine is an amino acid which accumulates as cells metabolize. Homocysteine causes the cells to break down, thus making them more susceptible to invasion by foreign pathogens. Diseases of many varieties can thereby invade and destroy cells. An intake of daily nutrients specifically; 500mg of Vitamin B12, 800 mcg of Folic Acid, 25 mg of Vitamin B6, 25 mg of Riboflavin and 500 mg of TMG (trimethylglycine) removes the homocysteine from the cells. Sears believes that daily consumption of seven antioxidants specifically; Vitamin A, Vitamin E, Vitamin C, Alpha Lipoic Acid, CoQ10, Lutein and Lycopene assist in fighting the deleterious effects of free radicals. The free radicals are by-products of the oxidative process; in essence free radicals destroy cells. Antioxidants work to remove free radicals from the cells, thus preserving the cell.

In their compendium on drugs entitled "The Pharmacological Basis of Therapeutics", Louis Goodman and Alfred Gilman" provide a detailed overview of drugs so that one can begin to understand the complexity of chemical agents and their effects on the human body. Seniors may not be ready to undertake an exhaustive and detailed study of pharmacology but may seek to understand the contraindications of drugs by doing some online search before they begin to self-administer drugs. Consultation with a medical expert or naturopath might ensure the proper evaluation of a drug, prior to including it in one's diet.

Goodman and Gilman have stipulated that any chemical agent that is foreign to the body is classified as a drug. These agents can have some effect on the physiological system. This would infer that any substance other than a saline solution identical in property to that found in one's body, is a drug. For example, any substance including coffee, tea, hot chocolate, sport drinks, vitamins, minerals or herbal substance would be included as drugs. Depending on their molecular structure and chemical composition, these would produce predictable side effects on the body. Goodman and Gilman have noted all liquid, food products or chemical substances ingested can act at specific cellular sites within the body. The amount of the drug taken, the concentration, the rate of absorption, distribution, ability to bind with other chemicals, localization in tissues, biotransformation and excretion are other factors which must be considered in order to understand the effect of drugs on the human body. Therefore, anyone who is about to embark on the systematic usage of chemicals whether it be in liquid form, food, vitamin, mineral supplements, or herbal medicines need to seek out consultation with specialists in the pharmaceutical field to ensure they are not harming themselves.   There are many ways of ensuring good health. One way is to consult Canada's Food Guide (www.healthcanada.gc.ca/foodguide). I will not spend a great amount of time on the foods which are important for optimal health. This guide describes the recommended four food groups:

1) vegetables/fruit.
2) grain products.
3) milk and alternatives.
4) meat and alternatives.

Furthermore, the number of servings per food group is included for the consumer. The most important piece of advice is that food should be in its natural state. The more processed the food is, the lesser it is of benefit to one's health.

LIQUIDS:
Liquids are necessary for the survival of the human species. The human body is 98 percent liquid. One must strive to maintain homeostatic balance, otherwise dehydration can occur. Thirst is a primary drive state and the motivation to seek liquid substances is inherent in one's drive for survival. The area in the brain known as the lateral hypothalamus when electrochemically stimulated motivates the human to seek out liquids to satisfy this craving. Once satiated, the person discontinues drinking. In this manner, a homeostatic (balanced) relationship can ensure the survival of the organism. Liquids need to be consumed by humans and lower organisms to ensure survival. Many liquid substances have been researched and it is imperative the senior understand this knowledge so they become aware of the underlying biochemical properties. Often, one is informed they should consume certain products but little time is spent in the evaluation of the chemical effects of these products on the body. Below, I have included an overview of some liquids so the reader can be apprised of the benefits of these on longevity.

WATER:
One can never get enough water. This substance has no calories and can easily quench thirst. Physiologists indicate humans need a vast quantity of water so they can re-hydrate. There is a continual loss of water through usage at the cellular level, perspiration and excretion. Water is necessary and essential for physical well-being. The source of water is also of utmost importance because an abundance of heavy metals can lead to toxicity thereby decreasing longevity. At

one time, it was thought that bottled water would provide the individual with a healthy and quick source for consumption. But now, one comes to realize   plastic used in water bottles contains high levels of bisphenol A. Frequent use of plastic water bottles can lead to deleterious health problems. One has to be cautious in their use of readily available liquids because the source or the container used to store the product can have an adverse effect on one's health. There are many contaminants in tap water, bottled water, lake water or well water. Furthermore, many chemical additives such as fluoride or chlorine which are used to reduce bacterial/parasitic/viral content can have negative effects on one's health.

BEER:
There has been much written about beer. It would appear from recent research that one of the greatest advantages of beer is the fact it contains silicon. This substance not only promotes bone formation but it also prevents bone loss. In essence, silicon assists in strengthening bones in the human body, thereby warding off osteoporosis. The research on beer, likely funded by Beer Companies would indicate that not all beer is created equal. One must consume beer that has a high content of malt and hops; these ingredients provide a larger amount of silicon. As the senior person ages, there is a greater need for more silicon. For the most part, silicon can be obtained through natural sources including porridge, granola cereals, bananas, multi-grain bread, carrots, and raisins. The daily dose of silicon obtained from food is about 25 milligrams. Older people however need about 50 milligrams of silicon. This translates to about one litre (3 bottles) of a high

quality silicon beer per day, if one is not obtaining silicon in a daily diet. I am not advocating that seniors commence imbibing three beers a day, but use it as an additive when they fail to consume a daily dosage of silicon through natural food products. According to research, silicon is a useful substance because it not only wards off osteoporosis but also improves elasticity of the skin and allows for healthy growth of teeth, gums and bones.

WINE:
Over the centuries, many cultures have used wine in their diet; they have had fewer incidents of health related disorders. A comparison of the French culture with that of the British Isles has shown that both countries have a high level of fat consumption in their diets. The French however, do not have as many cardiovascular related disorders. Investigation has found the only difference between these cultures is their wine consumption. The French apparently, use copious amounts in their diet whereas those from the British Isles have a lower consumption of wine. Research would indicate that wine contains a special by-product known as resveratrol. This polyphenolic compound appears to be at the basis of the beneficial property of wine. Specific grapes including the muscadine varieties have higher concentrations of the chemical resveratrol. During fermentation of grapes in the wine making process, the skins of the grape produce the resveratrol. Red wine it appears has a much greater concentration (160ug) of resveratrol, in comparison to other foods (ie. red grapes, peanuts). Research would indicate that moderate usage of wine and the by-product resveratrol is of benefit in

reducing coronary heart disease. Furthermore, resveratrol has antioxidant properties which have been positively associated with the inhibition of free radicals, the chemicals at the basis of cell aging. Much research is being garnered on the benefits of resveratrol. Some investigators have found that red wine aids in digestion, and acts as a antimicrobial agent against pathogenic oral streptococci bacteria involved in tooth decay. Other research with lower organisms has found that resveratrol because of its high level of polyphenols has chemoprevention properties which assist in combating cancer tumours, diabetes, obesity, and food borne pathogens. As more research is completed on resveratrol, the added benefits of moderate wine consumption will prove of use to the aging population. One to two glasses daily are good for one's health and longevity.

Refer to Appendix 1: A Detailed Analyses of Natural Food, Herbal Substances and Pharmaceutical Drugs are Outlined in this Section.

CHAPTER FIVE

MID LIFE CRISIS: DON'T GET STRESSED OUT

Rule #7: Stressed out people age faster.

Any event which presents conflict in life will evoke stress and anxiety. Midlife is the period between 40 to 60 years of age. According to Erik Erikson, it is during this time the individual seeks to generate some meaningful activity. For some, this period is used to establish oneself in a profession, and for others this culminates with raising a family. Once these goals are achieved, some adults evaluate their role as they attempt to establish the next meaningful part of their life.

Once children leave the family home, middle aged people struggle with the "empty nest syndrome". Some flounder unable to gain direction in their lives because of the loss of their role in caring for their children. Those who find themselves in this predicament, undergo a midlife crisis. Some make adjustments and return to interests generated before their families took precedent in their lives, whereas others become depressed and seek out psychological intervention. Counselling can assist middle age people in their transition to the next phase of their lives. Not all people deal with mid life crises in a similar manner. To some, new found freedom allows them to move to the next stage.

For those who can not adjust to the changes created by midlife, there is a need to evaluate their underlying stress. Earlier in this book, I introduced some of the research undertaken by Hans Selye. He believed that adaptation to an ever changing environment was one of the most important physiological, psychological adjustments a person would make during a lifetime. Selye maintained that humans must have the ability to adjust to external events in order to adapt and survive. The inability to adapt would only lead to stress related disorders including heart disorders, cancer and other life altering ailments. Essentially the inability to adapt could lead to one's demise.

Hans Selye viewed stress as a non-specific response to any physical or psychological stressor. Stressors included a multitude of events including physical (temperature), psychological (demands at work), or social (retirement) which could have an impact on the individual. Whatever the event, stress mediates changes in the host. The emotional centre in the brain known as the hypothalamus relays incoming messages so that a state of preparedness can ensue. The hypothalamus releases a chemical messenger to undertake this role. This hormone informs the autonomic nervous system to release catecholamines (adrenalin), or ACTH to release hydroxycorticosteroids (cortisol). Adrenalin is needed on a short term basis and cortisol on a long term basis to prepare the body to cope with the incoming stressor.

Stressful events, whether environmental, psychological, or social, can lead to underlying physiological reactions.

The length of time the body continues to release hormones after the stressor has been experienced will determine the impact on the body. For example, death in the family is perceived as a negative social event. The reaction experienced, will depend on the individual's ability to cope with their grief. Research shows the average individual will require approximately a year to cope with the death of a loved one.

Many Hollywood movies use these themes in their scripts. For example, in the film "About Schmidt" the viewer begins to understand that Schmidt's life is thrown into turmoil because of life changes. Warren Schmidt (Jack Nicholson) is just about to retire and has made some post-retirement plans. These plans however are thrown into disarray following the death of his wife. At first, he flounders because his life has undergone a drastic transition. Much like any person undergoing stress, Warren Schmidt shows the typical stage of shock which is followed by depression. He makes an attempt to resist the negative impact by undertaking a set of plans. Errors in judgement however, cause some troublesome experiences for him, but Schmidt eventually learns to cope with his two major stressors, the death of his wife and his retirement. He begins to pursue other avenues in order to fulfil some of his dreams. He comes to believe that he is now better off because he doesn't have to deal with work and its daily routines. His wife's quirks, especially her nattering, heavy use of facial creams, and obsession with his bathroom habits have all added to his stress. Over the years these situations had created frustration and anger for him. Like any person undergoing a negative event, Schmidt learns to rely on his defense mechanisms. He rationalizes the negative events in his life, so that he can offset the stress experienced because of these untimely stressors. To re-build his own inner self, Schmidt must restructure his psyche. This transition allows Schmidt to find himself. By the end of the film Schmidt has moved to another level of adjustment. He comes to terms with his identity as he explores the environment beyond his marital relationship and the confines of his office. Warren Schmidt learns to cope with his new found independence. The emotional pain of his transition from the loss of his job and his wife permits him to metamorphosize into a better and stronger person.

In life there are many negative stressors, each has to be carefully evaluated. At midlife, one must strive for balance. Chinese philosophy describes this in the concept of Yin and Yang. Events occur in life for a reason. There is always a positive to every negative event. For example, during midlife one's chance of incurring a physiological disorder (ie. cardio-vascular disease) increases. After experiencing a heart attack, a period of hospitalization allows for recuperation. While undergoing later medical evaluation, the patient learns their myocardial infarct was caused because of blockage in the arteries. Heart surgery is undertaken to repair the damage. In time, the patient learns to take better care of their health through diet and exercise. It serves no purpose to get stressed about the event. One must learn to accept the incident as a positive event. The victim becomes apprised of their diseased heart and must make some life changes. To recover from this tragic event, the patient must undertake a plan to make better choices. These changes in lifestyle, place the individual at less risk for future disease. Many people die from massive coronary arrests. Having had a heart attack, the patient learns that reparative surgery is a step in the recovery process. There are some negatives to every event but positives also emerge; one learns to incorporate these into their future plans for better health.

Some years prior, I conducted research on patients who had undergone open heart surgery. The participants were evaluated with personality tests and placed in two respective groups; Type A and Type B based upon their previous lifestyle. Research undertaken by Allan Glasser and his colleagues had shown that people who had been high driving and aggressive (Type A) were more prone to myocardial infarcts than less goal oriented and less aggressive people (Type B). In a later study conducted by myself and Bert Leith, we found that Type A and Type B personality characteristics were not correlated with myocardial infarct. What we did find from our study was that Type A and Type B patients who had experienced heart attacks and received surgery had elevated levels of depression following their post operative recovery. One would have expected the patients who had survived a heart attack, would be elated. These patients however commiserated about their unfortunate circumstances and felt much self-pity.

To offset their depression and negative evaluation of this life altering experience, I implemented relaxation training exercises coupled with cognitive-behavioral group therapy. In time, many of the patients began to view the beneficial aspects of their illness rather than wallow in self-pity. They were reminded that longevity can be short if one does not take care of their health. This study taught me that people have a difficult time coping with major stressors and the altering effects on their life. Many suffer from post-traumatic anxiety following serious mishaps, and often psychological intervention is needed to assist patients in recovering from these emotional wounds. It is imperative that people who have experienced major stressors are provided with counselling/therapy to explore their underlying behavioral or psychological concerns.

Positive coping during the senior years is of importance to one's health. Sometime after the age of 50, many people will retire. Some will adjust well to their new found freedom whereas others will face midlife crises. The process of coping involves both the planning and undertaking of specific activities. The senior who plans for retirement, must prepare for the experience so an adjustment can be made to cope with the demands. Through positive strategies, the individual attempts to gain control of their lives. For example, the news of the death of a loved one can induce stress. Any significant loss of life causes trauma and is experienced as such by family members. However, if one begins to understand that the process of aging invariably leads to death, then the stage becomes a natural progression of life events. The positive aspect of aging would be the realization that one's life has been of some importance. Having pursued a profession, raised a family and passed on values to children would be tantamount to Erik Erikson's concept of generativity. During the generativity stage, one strives to accomplish something in their lives. In later years, the senior begins to accept the fact they will eventually die. This acceptance reduces the anxiety and panic of this emotional process. Once a person begins to understand the process of aging by showing acceptance of death, then the anxiety pertaining to this event creates less stress for the person. No one wishes to undergo a lengthy painful illness prior to death. Any incapacitation or subsequent palliative care creates anxiety for not only the victim but also the family members. At the final stage of life, death becomes a positive event if the recipient does not have to experience worry, fear or pain. Chronologically, many humans have the physiological ability to live until 80 years. To exist beyond this time in a healthy manner is in actuality a privilege but can become mired in negative consequences including illness, and incapacitation.

There are many ways that people can psychologically prepare themselves for health crises in later life. One of primary means is by talking with loved ones. In her work on death and dying, Elisabeth Kubler-Ross described five stages of grief that one goes through as they face the inevitable experience known as death. When one learns they have a disease or terminal illness the natural response is shock, followed by denial, anger, bargaining, depression, seeking solutions, and last acceptance of death. Seniors who have had a fulfilling life may not always go through this same process. Unlike those who are faced with an untimely demise, healthy seniors who have had the chance of maximizing their lives can learn to cope effectively with their later years. Many seniors have fulfilled their life's dreams and come to an acceptance of death by the end of their life cycle.

After the age of 50, one should accept each day for what it is and attempt to maximize a hedonistic plan. There are important events we hope to accomplish before death. In the movie, "The Bucket List", Edward Cole (Jack Nicholson) faced with terminal illness decides to embark on experiences he has dreamt of but never undertaken. The reader is also introduced to Carter Chambers (Morgan Freeman) who shares the same hospital room with Edward Cole. The two men are world's apart in terms of their background; Chambers having worked as an auto mechanic most of his life; and Cole having achieved wealth through his entrepreneurial endeavors. The audience experience a sense of pathos towards these characters because of their terminal illness. These characters quickly transcend from denial to acceptance of their ultimate demise. Having only 3 to 6 months to live, Chambers and Cole embark upon an adventure which allows for self-discovery. The "Bucket List" becomes a self-regulated psychotherapy session in which Chambers and Cole begin to understand themselves, their lives and their eventual deaths. Their way of coping with death is to accept life as it unfolds which ultimately changes their destiny. Much like the control that one exerts in every day life, the purveyors of the "Bucket List" control their destiny. Rather than subjecting themselves to the contraindications of experimental medical treatment including chemotherapy and radiation, they take control of their final days on earth. The important lesson we learn from this film, is that faced with death, one does not have to sit back and accept the eventuality of death. One has to make the ultimate choice and that is to fulfil personal goals before death occurs.

Like many events in midlife, negative situations can either be a tragedy, or a road to self-discovery. There aren't any easy answers for those who must travel this road. It is imperative however, that seniors realize they have ultimate control of their lives. As masters of their destiny, seniors have to realize they can decide on their fate and embark on a path to fulfil their dreams.

Many seniors are content with their lives. During the summer months they spend time with their family and friends. When winter encroaches, they migrate to warmer climates in the southern states and happily pursue activities with friends. From my interaction with seniors I have found they like to take the path of least resistance. They prefer a simple lifestyle. Other than having to travel and relocate residences for the winter months, there is little that has to be done. Some seniors prefer little stress in their lives as they unwind during this final stage of life. Others however, do not perceive that a change from one residence to another in a warmer climate to be of importance. One man informed me that at 65 years of age, he still enjoyed the change in seasons and looked forward to the winter months so that he could cross-country ski and snowshoe. His wife not being as physically adventurous also enjoyed the changes in the season, but preferred to relax in the comfort of their home, sitting next to the fireplace with her favourite book. Another man 63 years of age indicated that he would never go to the southern climate during winter because to do so would indicate that he was ready to accept senescence. Also, he noted that his wife did not enjoy the warmth of the southern climate but preferred to stay home and engage in her handicrafts.

There are many ways of coping with midlife. To some, this period signifies a transition to the last phase of life as they prepare for death. To others, it is only the beginning of a new stage in which they can spend more time engaged in an activity. Preparation for the senior years is beneficial and can serve as a way of coming to terms with this phase. It is better to have a plan as opposed to merely exist as one awaits their imminent death. No one knows how much time they have on earth; it could be one day or it could be years. Perhaps we are all carded with a termination date or maybe it is merely chance or fate which leads to our demise. Being at the wrong place at the wrong time can lead to an unanticipated accident. It is better not to know when death is about to happen. Elisabeth Kubler-Ross found that people experience anxiety as they attempt to adjust to death. It is important for seniors to remember that death is only another milestone in their lifecycle.

CHAPTER SIX

HUMAN SEXUALITY

Rule #8: A healthy sex life knows no age boundaries.

Early Research:
An evaluation of human sexuality shows that we have come a long way since Sigmund Freud brought sexual behaviour out of the closet. The classic study by Alfred Kinsey, Wardell Pomeroy and Clyde Martin and the subsequent production of their book "Sexual Behavior in the Human Male" furthered our understanding of sexuality. In this book, one learns that males have varied sexual experiences; heterosexual behaviour being the predominant practise. Later research by the same authors and Paul Gebhard a statistician provided similar findings for females. In their book "Sexual Behavior in the Human Female", the authors discovered that females also engage in varied sexual practices. The pioneering work by the aforementioned authors was fraught with criticism, because of the lack of standardization in the collection of the data. Ostensibly, the sampling of subjects was not randomized but focused on interviews with college graduates who were apparently over repre-

sented in the sampling process.

Alfred Kinsey and his colleagues' research demonstrated that sexual mores are shaped by social and cultural values. Furthermore, this pioneering research brought the discourse on sexuality to the public domain. It set the pace for later exploration of this topic. By evaluating the sexual behaviours practised by people, it becomes apparent there were many varied sexual practises common in the USA in the 1940's and 1950's. Later evaluation of sexuality by William Masters and Virginia Johnson went one step further than subjective interviews. They evaluated the physiological bases of sexuality. To obtain a detailed understanding of what occurs prior to and during coitus, Masters and Johnson connected their subjects to an apparatus which measured physical changes which occurred during phases (ie. excitement, plateau, orgasm and resolution) of sexual activity. Their work showed few differences between males and females in sexual activity; the only difference being that females had multiple orgasms whereas men required a refractory period between orgasms. The refractory period in males varied in duration and was dependent on the age of the person; younger males at age 20 had a refractory period lasting minutes, whereas older males had a refractory period, lasting hours. Masters and Johnson's research noted that males and females were capable of sexual activity and orgasm well into their later years (ie. 70 and older).

Some researchers have evaluated the sexual behaviour of older females and males. Sheryl Kingsberg has noted that at midlife, heterosexual relationships are enhanced by factors including emotional intimacy, autonomy, management of stress and distractions. These variables tend to be the mitigating factors which allow one to achieve sexual balance. The quantity of sexual activity changes as one ages but not the quality of the sexual experience within a satisfying relationship. Sheryl Kingsberg believes the basis of sexual desire during senior years must be evaluated in terms of sexual drive, beliefs, values and motivation. Theorists have posited that as one ages, many psychological and physiological changes occur. According to Cindy Meston there is a greater decline in sexual interest and desire in aging women in comparison to aging men. Menopause and andropause signal that the aging person needs to slow down sexually.

Female Sexuality:
There are many physiological changes which women undergo after menopause. The decrease in hormonal activity, especially estrogen and progesterone are at the basis of this transition in women. In females, this leads to a loss of pubic hair, decrease in fat and subcutaneous tissue from the mons pubis, atrophy of the labia majora and shortening and loss of the elasticity in the vaginal barrel. In younger women, lubrication of the vaginal barrel requires about 15 seconds, however in postmenopausal women it generally takes at least 5 minutes and possibly longer for vaginal lubrication to occur. Other noticeable changes include thinning of the vaginal barrel because of decrease in cells which comprise the epithelial lining. This generally makes sexual intercourse painful for females.

Within the female gender the decrease in estrogen and progesterone signals the diminished production of egg cells. During the regular menstrual cycle, younger females have their greatest production of estrogen and progesterone at about the 14 to 16 day of their cycle. This coincides with the release of egg cells allowing for a greater chance of impregnation. At about day 12 to day 18, females tend to have their highest level of sexual arousability. This leads to higher motivation for sexual contact. Research has shown that females undergoing these changes subconsciously dress more provocatively in order to attract males. Furthermore, some researchers have found females at this stage tend to be more attracted to masculine males (ie. broader shoulders, larger pectoral muscles, rounder buttocks) possibly because they perceive men with these characteristics as being more virile.

At menopause, there is a diminution of the production and release of egg cells. This can occur in women as early as 45 years of age. In response, the aged female shows a diminished interest in sexual activity. Individual variability however would indicate that some women continue to produce eggs well into their fifties. Research has shown that after age 60, 56% of married women are still sexually active. For these women, the need for sexual activity is still elevated in comparison to those women who have reached early menopause. The decrease in testosterone, estrogen, and progesterone leads to loss in sexual libido. Ostensibly, testosterone levels decrease rapidly between the ages of 20 and 40 in females; with a slight loss between ages 60 to 80. At specific times during the aging process, women who have lowered interest in sexuality because of underlying changes in biochemistry can seek out medical intervention through the use of prescribed medication. Testosterone and tibilone (estrogen-progesterone-testosterone) substrates can be administered to women to increase sexual arousal. Administration of a testosterone substrate has other advantages for females. It apparently improves general well being, increases bone mineral density, muscle mass and decreases headaches and mastalgia (pain in mammary glands).

One must bear in mind that loss of sexual drive in women after age 50, is a result of post-menopausal conditions resulting from a decrease in estrogen, progesterone and testosterone. Left untreated, diminished production of these hormones will greatly affect the sex life of the aging female. According to research conducted by Margaret Nussbaum and her colleagues, older women especially those over the age of 65 report fewer sexual encounters. Factors cited for the reduction in sexual activity include lack of orgasm, lowered sexual interest, decline in lubrication, painful intercourse, and health related issues (ie. safe sex). Research by John Morley and his colleagues indicates that a decrease in sexual activity in older females is a result of physical and/or psychosocial factors. The physical factors include, vaginal dryness, menopause, dyspareunia (pain during intercourse), and decreased libido/orgasm. Psychosocial factors include safe sex, extramarital affairs, insufficient partners, sexual aversion, dysphoria and decreased libido/orgasm. One 65 year old female patient whom I met in my practise because of a depression issue, acknowledged that she had enjoyed a wonderful sex life with her spouse but at age 65, had experienced dyspareunia which greatly impacted on the enjoyment of sexual intercourse. The aversion caused by the pain made her feel less comfortable engaging in sexual intercourse, in time she avoided all sexual contact with her spouse because of the physical irritation and pain. She indicated that she had tried various lubricants sold in pharmacies but none seemed to reduce her pain.

Male Sexuality:
In the aging male, a decrease in androgen leads to andropause or the diminution of sexual activity. Research has shown that androgen levels begin to decrease by age 25 and by age 70 are only at 10 percent of the level they were during adolescence. Furthermore, research shows that between age 40 and 60, men experience a reduction in testosterone which leads to a reduction in sexual activity. Other associated psychological conditions include attitude change, mood change, fatigue, and loss of energy. These create many problematic issues for aging males. A good example of these changes are evident in the case of a colleague who at age 60 indicated that he had functioned at a high level in his profession. He noted that he experienced such a drastic change in mood because of diminished sexual arousal caused by andropause, that he had feelings of suicide ideation and contemplated ways of killing himself. After consultation with his physician, he received treatment for his depressed mood. Through the use of androgen therapy and antidepressant drugs to elevate his mood, he once again commenced functioning at an acceptable level.

There appears to be individual variability in the production of testosterone as the male ages. Some older males have such a high sex drive that they seek out younger females to satisfy their sexual cravings. Today, there are many reported situations of older men procreating with younger females. These males continue to produce high levels of testosterone because the gonado-stimulating-hormone is still in full productivity. For males who continue to have high production levels of testosterone, there may be a heightened need for sexual contact. The biological need for sex continues because of the higher production of underlying sex hormones which lead to higher production of testosterone. Those males who do not experience andropause at age 50, may continue to seek sexual activity well into their 80's. In fact, research has shown that by age 60, 75% of the males were still sexually active.

Recent studies have shown that some males experience sexual problems. Jonathan Levy undertook the Massachusetts Male Aging Study in the late 1980's. His research showed that 52% of men aged 40 to 70 had problems with impotence. At 40 years of age, 5% of the male population had complete impotence. By age 70, 15% of the males reported impotence. Many of the 1,709 males in this cross-sectional study were from varied backgrounds. Physical conditions which may have precipitated impotence included diabetes (7%), heart disease (12%), hypertension (30%) and smoking (22%). The data collected by Levy and his colleagues indicated that testosterone levels decreased in some males at age 25 and by age 40, 5% of men showed signs of andropause. In fact, Walter Bortz and Douglas Wallace found that in aged men, a decline in sexual activity is closely associated with erectile dysfunction, impotence, greater time spent in refractory phase, less ejaculate and a decrease in intensity of orgasm. These reported findings would indicate in aging males, sexuality can become problematic.

General Health and Sexual Issues:
Sexual activity is important for the well-being of intimate personal relationships during midlife. In his book, "Aging Well", George Vaillant notes that people who have satisfying sexual experiences during the senior years have healthier lifestyles and seem to be happier. But one must also consider the work of others especially that of Frank Beach and his colleagues who

evaluated sexual behaviour in lower organisms. Their research showed that too much exposure to the same subject caused sexual satiation. This is tantamount to the notion that too much exposure to the same stimulus decreases sexual attraction.

Humans interact on physical and psychosocial levels. Intimacy becomes an important variable which allows for relationships to grow over time. The aging population will continue to experience problematic sexual issues. As people get older, their need for sex generally diminishes. Problems arise however because of the timing of andropause and menopause. For couples who coincide in the onset of menopause or andropause, diminished sexual activity coincides with their biological needs. A relationship may not be dependent on continued sexual activity but on emotional and social needs. Some males and some females however do not reach andropause or menopause at the same time. These people may not be prepared to accept a diminution in sexual activity in their relationship. For males with a normal testosterone output there may be a biological need to continue engaging in coitus. Whereas some males may have a decreased output of testosterone but may not be willing to accept their biological fate and thus may seek out herbal aphrodisiacs or prescribed drugs (ie. Viagra, Cialis) as a way of enhancing their sex lives.

Conversely, some females who have not reached menopause may not be willing to accept erectile dysfunction of their partners. They may want their partners medically evaluated and treated so that sexual activity can be restored. Some females may insist their male partners commence taking prescribed drugs in order to rectify their sexual dysfunction. On the other hand, some females having reached menopause and having experienced a very low libido may not have any desire for sexual contact after menopause. They may not be willing to tolerate their partner's higher libido created by the use of prescribed drugs or aphrodisiacs. This could lead to problems in marital relationships especially where females are not willing to accept the enhanced sexual behaviour of their partners who are driven by artificial means.

According to Cindy Meston and Julia Heiman, the pain experienced during intercourse after menopause is due in part to the decreased vaginal lubrication and thinning of the vaginal lining. Evidence tends to suggest however that as soon as women implement the use of prescribed estrogen treatment or use lubricants they can return to a sexually satisfying relationship. Research is currently ongoing to evaluate the use of prescribed drugs for increased sexual libido in females. Ostensibly the drug ephedrine, a stimulant chemically similar in structure to amphetamine which is used as an appetite suppressant and to treat decongestion has been evaluated on sexual arousal in females. The results reported by Meston and Heiman would indicate that ephedrine can enhance female sexual arousal in the excitatory stage of activity. Although this study was experimental, the exploration of pharmacological application will undoubtedly lead to the discovery of new designer drugs to enhance sexual arousability in those females who seek treatment because of their sexual dysfunction.

This draws us back to the issue, "how much sex is enough"? What can couples or partners do when their mate is no longer sexually receptive because of diminished sex drive brought on by lowered level of a hormone. Should a partner, male or female be forced into sexual activity when there is a loss of interest brought on by physical or psychological factors?

Should a partner be coerced to engage in other forms of sexuality (ie. oral or manual stimulation) to fulfil their partner's needs when they are no longer interested? When a partner feels they do not have an obliging partner should they feel at ease in their decision to engage in self-stimulation (ie. masturbation) or should they feel little or no guilt in pursuing extra-marital relationships to satisfy their biological/sexual needs? Or should the partner be willing to accept their fate and take up hobbies (ie. exercise and fitness) to sublimate their sexual energies so they do not bring conflict to their marital arrangement?

There are many questions which emerge when one evaluates sexuality. According to motivation and emotion theorists, the human species has three primary drives. These include hunger, thirst and sexuality. Hunger and thirst are necessary for personal survival, whereas sexuality is only necessary for the survival of the species. If humans do not engage in sexual intercourse, the species would eventually cease to exist. From the time of early adolescence until later adulthood, there is a strong physiological need to mate. By engaging in coitus, humans inevitably procreate, and the species continue to flourish. The sexual drive in humans is so great that people show emotional discontent when they are not sexually active. They report volatile mood swings, including irritability, frustration and anger when their sexual needs are not being met. When healthy humans are not having sex, one can almost state they become miserable. Sex has always been a drive state amongst humans; they will continue to seek it on a regular basis. Lower organisms however are somewhat different from humans; their level of sexuality tends to be seasonal. It is highly correlated with environmental conditions which can provide for the survival of the species. Climate and food are seasonal variables which become pertinent factors for lower organism survival. In terms of sexuality, the human species is not climate dependent because their frontal brains allow them to plan for their needs. Sexual activity allows for procreation and it also serves as a recreational activity which many consider important for well-being of the person.

As one ages, the viability of egg cells and spermatozoa diminish, this can lead to unhealthy offspring. Thus from a physiological level, it would seem that sexual activity during the senior years is only necessary to provide pleasure, physical relief from tension of everyday life and to provide emotional comfort. Coitus in the senior years is not a necessity of life but a physical or psychological need which provides the partner with the confirmation of desirability and a sense of being wanted. Sexual involvement for seniors is more about emotional contact and bonding and less about the recreational pursuits achieved by younger people. Perhaps George Vaillant was correct when he suggested that older people who are healthier in the later years are happier because they obtain emotional comfort which is essential and necessary for one's well-being.

In his book, "Men Are From Mars, Women Are From Venus", Peter Gray posits that men and women are indeed a different species. Women thrive on emotional contact and support, whereas males are bound by the satisfaction of their physiological needs. Younger females seek out viable mates with healthy genes for procreation. There is some research which indicates that females show more interest in males who are physically attractive and have feminine characteristics. This indicates that women like socializing and dating males who are more female like in appearance. Perhaps these males have gotten in touch with their feminine side, known as the animus according to the theoretical notion posited by Carl Jung. When procreation enters the picture, females tend to show higher sexual attraction toward males with physical characteristics including large biceps, defined pectoral muscles (chests) and shapely gluteus maximus (butts). Unconsciously, one can only wonder whether some underlying primordial drive is at the basis of women's interest in males who physically appear to have better genetics.

The female species at specific times of their menstrual cycle, especially when they are ovulating at about day 14 to 16 make choices for mate selection. This is based upon the underlying estrogen, progesterone, and testosterone levels in their physiological systems. Research by Kristina Durante and her co-researchers have found that during ovulation, females apparently dress more seductively as a way of attracting prospective mates. Following the successful union of spermatozoa and egg cell, oxytocin release in females shuts down interest in sexual activity and the urge to mate. This allows the female time to care and bond with the offspring.

Women are a unique species who pursue sex with partners but are chemically bound by raising and nurturing their young. Through cultural mores, the human male appears to accept the females nurturing role. Human males have a sexual drive state from the time they reach pubescence and this lasts until senescence. Much of the male's energy seems to be directed toward the active pursuit of sexual partners. Michael Dunn and his colleagues evaluated partner selection through online dating services. They found that women tend to seek older and wealthier men as prospective mates. Conversely, men seek out relationships with females younger than themselves. Recently, in a conversation with an older male who had just reached his

90th birthday, he informed me that attractive younger females still caused him to become sexually aroused. However, he would quickly draw himself back to reality by telling himself that his interest in attractive younger females was not consistent with his physiological ability. He came to appreciate the sight of pretty younger women even though he could not do anything to wet his sexual appetite.

In the modern era, there has been some deviation from the norm in mate selection. Older women especially those with financial means or celebrity status, seek younger attractive men. This however appears to be a function of social status seeking and recreational sexual activity as opposed to a drive toward procreation. Research by Michael Dunn and colleagues has shown that women across all age groups and cultures seek out males of their own age group or somewhat older. This appears to be consistent with an evolutionary behaviour which indicates that females seek those with status, wealth and territorial rights. These factors increase the chances of their offspring having the best economic means for survival.

CHAPTER SEVEN

FINANCES AND LIFESTYLE IN RETIREMENT

Rule #9: Seniors must be conservative with their money.

People nearing retirement, must evaluate their financial status to ensure they will have a comfortable style in later years. In her article, "55 And You Haven't Saved A Dime", Liz Pulliam Weston indicates that if one reaches the age of 50 and hasn't saved for retirement, they will be in financial trouble. According to statistics collected from the 2009 Retirement Confidence Survey - by the Employee Benefit Research Institute (EBRI), 30% of workers age 55 and older indicated they had less than $10,000 saved for retirement. According to the EBRI, by age 55 a person who earns approximately $40,000 a year has to set aside 27% of their income to retire at 65. A person earning $60,000 should have saved 33%; while someone earning $80,000 should have saved 37%; and someone who makes $100,000 would have to save 40% to ensure a comfortable retirement. The reality of the numbers game is that many people will not have saved enough money to retire early. According to Pulliam Weston one's best strategy for retirement is working as long as possible. By offsetting one's retirement's age to 70, instead of 65 will allow the person, to earn and save more money which can be contributed toward retirement funds; these funds can then grow over a longer period of time. By using these strategies, the individual will have more time to save for their retirement. By delaying retirement until 70, allows one to reduce their yearly retirement contributions.

The North American population has continued to age and a large increase in baby boomers will occur until the middle of the 21st Century. There will be much pressure on Government agencies to provide old age security benefits to the aging populace. Although many would like to retire at 55, this will not be a reality. Many people post 55 will have to remain in the work force. With the removal of mandatory retirement, older people will continue to stay within the ranks of working adults. This will assist in stabilizing the economics of old age security benefits. However, by age 55 many seniors will not have the physical energy or the motivation to continue working. Many older people will only want to work part-time whereas others will continue to work because of their economic needs or personal interests. People are not alike in their levels of health, or their interest in working after age 55. These variables alone will be the mitigating factors which will either lead one to retire or not retire.

A recent investigation by Karen Holden and her colleagues showed that 29.7% of elderly people have experienced financial distress because their income was below the poverty level during retirement years. Not only were these people economically disadvantaged but financial strain contributed to a decreased level of well-being in this elderly population. Financial difficulties create feelings of dependency, diminished self-worth, depression and somatic complaints in older people. Furthermore, Neal Krause and his colleagues have found that financial pressure creates loss of control in the elderly who somehow feel they are at the mercy of the social environment. It appears that the greater one values financial success, the greater their level of stress when they fail to achieve their goals of financial independence.

Some researchers have found that economically advantaged retirees are those who have double the income of those at the poverty level. In terms of demographics, the financially advantaged in retirement, are those who had stable jobs during the period of economic expansion after World War 2. Financially advantaged people have better education than their parents and have a better retirement lifestyle. Most are married, are home owners and have good community stability. Their income is generally received from multiple sources including company pensions, retirement savings plans and annuities. Overall, this group seems to have achieved a successful style because of an advantaged social and economic lifestyle achieved through hard work, financial planning and some luck.

Susan Higginbottom and her colleagues believe that one's retirement experience has an indirect effect on sense of purpose. This appears to create satisfaction and meaningfulness in life. By enhancing the retiree's skills, there is the chance that one can continue to work in some meaningful way after retirement. The senior workforce however is not always comprised of people who work into their later years because of interest in their jobs. For example, in my travels to the southern States I have often interacted with elderly men and women employed as packagers and carry-outs in grocery stores. I've asked these people their reason for working beyond age 50. Many admit needing the extra money to survive the economic times, whereas others admit they have undertaken these jobs because they were bored sitting at home. I have also encountered elderly people in Canada working in similar positions. These people tell me that prior to retirement they had high paying jobs. After retirement they accepted lower paying jobs so they could occupy some of their free time. They work in these positions for many reasons but their primary one is boredom following retirement. By engaging in a simple job, allows the senior social contact with others, a purpose in life and some extra money.

Bernice Neugarten has researched the concept of disengagement from the workforce. She stated that as one becomes disengaged there has to be other avenues to hold one's interests. Those who don't disengage from work successfully become candidates for physical and psychological ailments. We know from the literature in this area, that successful disengagement isn't an easy task. People tend to believe that they have a plan in mind but this gradually falls apart within the first year of retirement. To assist seniors in financial planning many agencies including banks and financial security companies offer financial pre-retirement planning seminars to seniors.

Michal Mor-Barat and his colleagues would agree that several factors lead the elderly to work beyond retirement years. These include an aging work force, the decline of young people entering the labour force, increased life expectancy and insufficient retirement funds. An investigation of psychological well-being of people employed in partial employment showed they have sense of purpose, direction and creation of social networks because of their jobs. These people go to work each day rather than face the mundane experience of sitting at home and doing nothing. People need to be busy and need social interaction. Many people who choose to work after retirement are looking to stimulate their minds and this can be accomplished in a setting where there is some cognitive challenge.

Following retirement, many people who become disengaged from the workforce find it difficult to meet friends. They don't have particular strategies nor do they have any involvement in social groups which allow them to meet others. One retired man informed me during a counselling session that he knew of many "buddies" who lived in his community. His problem was his inability to approach them because he had limited contact with them over the past twenty years of his life. I informed him that he should think of a mutual interest. This client mentioned that he and his friends had liked fishing prior to their estrangement caused by work and family commitments. I informed him to organize a fishing trip, setting out all particulars prior to asking them to attend. He contacted an outfitter and inquired about a three day fishing trip to Northern Ontario. When he contacted his friends, he had no trouble getting affirmative replies from them. This client informed me that his friends had a wonderful time on the trip. They were able to reminisce past adventures. The event was so successful that all agreed on a yearly outing.

People seek social involvement with others. Friendships have no boundaries. True friends can re-unite at some point in their later lives. Often, it is just a matter of making contact. Many people have a social awkwardness but once the "ice is broken" they begin to feel relaxed and are able to partake of the new found relationships.

If one were to rank two of the most important factors necessary for a reasonable retirement they would be health and financial security. In her article, "Boomers Put Health at Top of Retirement Priorities", Chaya Cooperberg has noted that a vast majority (67%) of baby boomers are in agreement that health was more important than money (23%). Most people do not perceive retirement as a negative event. It only becomes negative if one does not have the health or the finances to maintain an expected style of life. For example, if the retiree once had an annual income of $60,000 dollars to provide for their sustenance but now have to subsist on $20,000, some hardship will be imposed. Conversely, if one has accrued sufficient income through pension and investments they should have a positive framework to pursue retirement. People who have good health and finances look forward to retirement. In contrast, those with sound finances and ill health don't feel good about forced retirement. It appears that poor health does become an issue in retirement. Frank Sammartino has found that approximately 17% of the population between the ages 60 to 67 will retire because of poor health. When one retires because of ill health, there is generally a consensus to accept whatever retirement package that is available in order to provide for one's sustenance.

There are some seniors of retirement age who have not had positive circumstances. Bad luck, economic hardship, poor planning or combined factors have led to poor retirement status. When one has many hardships especially ill health and poor finances, Pat Keith believes there is a tendency to have a less resourceful and productive retirement. The inability to get ahead based upon misfortune is a theoretical model evaluated by Julian Rotter, in his internal/external locus of control model. This model infers that some individuals believe their fate is attached to external factors beyond their control. When these factors arise in life, they cause unpredictable events to occur. Many people in society today value control over their lives. When circumstances arise which cause disadvantage, people tend to blame the external forces (ie. bad luck) for their losses.

In the 1970's, many financial vehicles including RRSP's were created to give the average Canadian citizen ways of deferring tax payments to the government. These particular vehicles have allowed Canadians to defer paying taxes on their salary. Some concerns arise with RRSP's because one is limited to the amount of money they can defer on a yearly basis. Equally disturbing to many people on the verge of retiring is the news that financial resources guaranteed by government agencies including the Canada Pension Plan are depleting rapidly because of the influx of baby boomers. Those facing retirement are concerned that as the economy in North America deteriorates, one's level of financial security will also erode.

The question that many face today pertains to a retirement plan for the future. Will retirees have money available to pay for basic living including food and shelter? Who will pay contributions to the government plan? At the federal government level, many changes are taking place to provide funds for old age security. These include upping the age of retirement from 65 to 67 in Canada. At this writing many Americans work until they are in their early seventies. When one evaluates historical cases, it is interesting to note that in the 1980's the Canadian Supreme Court ruled that it was against one's rights to work beyond 65 years. Ostensibly, it was believed that people over 65 years of age were somehow unable to cope with the demands of employment. I recall the case of an associate professor at Laurentian University taking his case all the way to Supreme Court so that he could prolong his employment. Physically, he believed himself capable of teaching well and receiving favourable evaluations from his students. Much to his chagrin, this professor was mandated "too old to work" in the university setting. He was asked to leave on the grounds of a Supreme Court ruling. One must question to what extent the government will impose forced choices. By some draconian measure will some retirees now be required to return to work because their skills are in demand?

What financial strategies can we use as we near retirement? In his book "The Wealthy Barber", David Chilton offers many strategies to assist with preparation for retirement. According to his statistics, 50 percent of the Canadian population won't have sufficient funds for retirement. Chilton does provide some common sense approaches toward financial strategies which will assist one during retirement. People approaching age 50 should heed his advice. The tips which I found most beneficial include investing in RRSPs, RESPs, Pension funds and saving a portion of one's weekly/monthly salary. Having a salaried job over a 30 year period, utilizing some financial strategies and common sense, will assist many people to ease into their retirement years without financial distress.

One senior friend who travelled with us on our yearly outdoor events must have been on the same wavelength as

David Chilton because he had many strategies for successful aging. Bill's financial plan included saving 5 cents of every after tax dollar he made. When Bill was in his early thirties, he indicated there were few financial avenues available so he decided on his own retirement plan. This allowed him to accrue considerable wealth over his life time. When he retired at age 67, his financial status allowed for a comfortable lifestyle. Bill's notion of financial strategizing was consistent with David Chilton's advice to "pay oneself first". By saving a small percentage of one's salary on a regular basis, allows for a sound financial plan for the future. By devising a plan, one embarks on a voyage toward financial security. Without a plan for accruing money, the senior will be left to depend on old age security benefits. This will undoubtedly be insufficient to allow for a comfortable lifestyle in the years beyond retirement.

It would seem that a limited number of seniors gain benefits from the Canadian social class structure. Those in the upper echelon who have businesses and tax write-offs appear to have the most stable finances and pensions available upon retirement. Those who worked diligently and have income within the $50,000 to $100,000 dollar range are taxed heavily. They are at an advantage however since they have money that can be invested in RRSPs. This can assist in deferring taxes and saving money for retirement years. There are others however who work in low paying jobs who have limited funds for investment. Their wages merely cover basic sustenance. Those with limited finances include the working poor, women who are widowed and/or residing alone. These people need special strategies in order to economically survive.

One senior explained that she devised a strategy for retirement. Estelle maintained that she was never able to save much money during her life because she was a stay at home mom with responsibilities to her family. She had remained in the home to raise her children and did not achieve financial independence. Her husband worked in a labour position but did not have a company retirement plan or savings to invest in RRSP's. Estelle returned to work as a teacher for approximately 15 years after her last child entered high school. Saving strategies were maximized and her house mortgage paid off. When her husband died, she had sufficient funds to maintain the household. At age 65 Estelle retired. She now receives her teaching pension and government subsidies. In combination with the funds she and her deceased spouse accrued during their working lives, she is able to subsist at a reasonable level. In Estelle's mind, her focus is now directed toward financial independence. She is frugal with her money because of the forced nature of her situation. Estelle does not have excessive retirement funds. She spends her time doing arts and crafts at a local community resource centre. She takes advantage of the low fees that she has to pay for joining community organizations. Estelle seeks out discounts offered to retirees. She attends free lectures on nutrition, health, and she exercises with other seniors. Through her activities, Estelle has been able to meet new friends and is socially and physically engaged in her community.

Barbara Logue has found that women workers in the population are more financially disadvantaged than men in their earnings and private pension coverage. It seems that when women retire from the workforce, they have had less time in employment and consequently have fewer social security benefits to draw on. Logue's research would indicate that in the early years of retirement approximately one in six of unmarried women have financial difficulties because of insufficient income. This places them in a desperate financial class as they live at the poverty level of existence. If their spouse's die they are faced with financial hardship.

One has to learn to be creative and solution focused in order to cope with retirement. Many seniors spend much time worrying about their financial status and therefore are unable to take advantage of the resources that are available to them. As this book is being completed, the economy in the USA and Canada is in a state of flux. Many people in the USA are losing their homes because of unemployment and heavy debt. In many cases, their houses are worth less on the real estate market than the mortgages being paid for the property. Many Canadians are in a better financial position than their American counterparts. Canada's federal old age security benefits still exist to assist with economic needs. Seniors have had to become more aware of the resources available in the community in order to survive this tumultuous period.

Recently, I read with interest that the American federal government was looking at a way of taxing wealthy USA citizens who renounce their American citizenship and choose to reside in tax free havens. It would seem that those who attempt to leave the country will have to pay tax on capital gains exceeding $600,000 USD. Considering that approximately only 1% of the American population comprises this group, the working class who earn about $60,000 a year or less will still have to bear the brunt of taxes.

Similar scenarios exist for wealthy Canadians who renounce their Canadian citizenship. These individuals travel to tax free countries and live in relative obscurity without paying any taxes on assets they have acquired. In his book "Take Your Money, And Run", Alex Doulis, a retired securities analyst recommends retiring to a tax free haven. By removing funds from RRSP's, paying penalties and then taking money with them to offshore havens, seniors can avoid further taxation. This appears simple enough to the wealthy person who has financial independence accrued from investments, pension plans and other savings vehicles. For the working class person however, this is not possible. It takes money to make money and most North Americans don't have surplus funds to invest. A small percentage of self-made millionaires exist, and not everyone will win a lottery.

What is the best strategy for those who don't have excessive finances? Financial wizards will tell you that the best and wisest choice is to pay off the home mortgage as soon as possible. If one lives within their means, a primary residence should be paid before 50 years of age. This will free up at least 15 years in which one can save money for retirement. Many Canadians believe they should have a cottage as well as a primary residence. The advice of the financial gurus is to forego the cottage until your main residence is paid. The interest paid over the period of one's mortgage is substantially increased when one has to pay two mortgages. The best adage for the retiree is to simplify life and exist within one's financial means. Only spend money on the things you need, not the things you want. Save the extra money and maximize your investments in RRSPs during retirement, and in RESPs for your children or grandchildren to ensure their future.

To maintain a reasonable level of existence in retirement, a senior requires a number of strategies. These include steady employment, wise spending, good saving habits, stable marital relationships, sound health and luck. Many middle class people make it to retirement years with all of the above in their favour. They are able to enjoy a middle class existence. Emotional and mental stability equips one to advance in life in a positive direction. There are some setbacks which can lead to problematic issues from time to time. Depending upon one's country of residence, there are always bureaucrats who tend to prey on tax paying citizens by imposing tax to usurp one's style of life. The only strategy for retirees who face this dilemma is through overt opposition to imposed tariffs. Bureaucrats in their wisdom do not always examine the individual style of life of retirees but tend to measure them as a group. Statistics reveal that many retirees because of sound employment and wise investment strategies have amassed a collective fortune in retirement funds. This represents a source of revenue for the political bureaucrats. When politicians attempt to tax these savings, retirees must protest and select "grey leaders" who will assist in fighting tariffs levelled at the retired class.

CHAPTER EIGHT

HOUSING AND RETIREMENT COMMUNITIES

Rule #10: Seniors need comfortable housing arrangements.

Retirement holds a special meaning for seniors as they plan to leave the workforce. The problem with retirement is that many people can not afford to disengage because of their economic situation. With retirement comes the added burden of limited monetary funds which precipitates a change in lifestyle. Every retiree must decide on the best strategy for their lifestyle change. A discussion on this topic with my colleague Ed Willauer, an economics professor indicated that seniors need to continue working as long as they are physically possible. If a senior can perform their job effectively he or she should remain in their job. This will ensure sufficient retirement funds through pension, savings or other investments to enable the senior to exist in a reasonable lifestyle. Longevity for most in North America is somewhere between 80 to 90 years of age.

    I look forward to retirement. Good timing, luck or being at the right place at the right time worked in my favour.

Like many others from the middle class, having a favourable steady job with a good wage has provided for my needs. There are many people in the workforce however who haven't been as lucky. These are people of the disadvantaged class who through no fault of their own find themselves facing retirement without adequate funds. This segment of the population weren't as lucky. They did not obtain proper education, employment, or get the breaks which would have ensured a decent retirement status. Women who remained at home to care for their young, the economically disadvantaged, the underemployed, emotionally distraught or the cognitively challenged are all part of this suffering group. Unlike the middle class, they will have a difficult time surviving the economic hardships of retirement.

During retirement, one's pension is dependent whether their company has a pension plan and this is based on the years of service. Most people who have a pension plan can estimate about 35% to 50% of what they earned during their best years of employment. Many will not have any pension plan and some will have limited funds in their pension plan. This will create financial hardship as they attempt to provide for housing, food, and ancillary expenses. Many will find themselves dependent on the Canada Pension Plan, Old Age Security or Guaranteed Income Supplement. The money one has accrued over their working lifetime will determine their style of life during the retirement years.

Information which I have researched indicates that seniors will have to make a decision regarding four particular options pertaining to housing as they exit the workforce:

1) Independent Housing: A decision will have to be made to reside in ones' home, condo, or apartment. This

arrangement will require that the senior be physically capable of undertaking repairs and maintenance. They will have to be prepared to shop and prepare their meals. There are many seniors who will choose to reside in their homes and they will do well in this particular arrangement.

2) Multiunit Complex: In this setting, the senior maintains their own living quarters possibly a room or small apartment within the complex. The person is provided with a range of services which could include meals, laundry and pharmaceutical dispensary so they don't have to travel outside of the complex to obtain these necessities. This is a beneficial arrangement for seniors especially those who don't have the physical ability to provide for their needs. Many seniors would enjoy this option because they maintain their autonomy and independence but have access to services. In this setting, it would be easy to continue friendships and engage in social activities with others.

3) Residential Community with Continued Care: This type of setting requires careful consideration because the costs are generally expensive; ones pension and retirement savings will have to be significant to pay for the services. It is imperative that a person has adequate funds. Often the senior is able to gain admittance to these facilities only to learn, they have insufficient funds over the long term to pay for their residency. One middle aged lady indicated that her father having reached the age of 80 and being a widower, decided upon relocation to a good quality residential community. With the proceeds from the sale of his home and his retirement pension averaged over a 10 year period, he barely had the funds to cover the $17,000 dollar yearly cost. Apparently, yearly costs were geared to a cost of living index, and

this could increase over time. In the event her father couldn't pay she would have to take money from her own pension fund to pay for her father's care.

4) Nursing Home: The last option is the one most seniors fear. When the senior can no longer function on their own, there is a need for continued care. This setting creates anxiety for most seniors because re-location to this type of facility infers the senior is in their final stage of life, and essentially preparing for death. Most seniors aren't ready to admit they are on their death bed. At the basis of the human psyche, are defense mechanisms. Denial seems to be used heavily by seniors as they reach the final stage of life. When the senior can no longer get out of bed, function on their own, or need ambulatory care to go to the washroom, they generally come to the realization that death is inevitable. Every senior who is at the final stage of life should be prepared to get their paper work in order. Wills need to be written and final plans necessary so unnecessary burden is not placed on family members. It is better to engage in positive reflection at this stage as noted from Erikson's writings rather than go to one's grave disparagingly.

Let us return to Option 1, Independent Housing. This book is about life after 50, and I will spend some time examining this option, because at retirement it is the most preferred choice. Most retirees can only afford one house and generally chose to remain in their current home. Government and Private Agencies have emerged to assist with this arrangement. Professionals known as "Certified Aging-In-Place Specialists" are available to assist seniors in making these plans.

Earlier in my career, I researched the effects of

housing options on seniors. Our findings showed that seniors expect options will be available at retirement. These include the following:

> 1) Location of housing and proximity to family and friends.
> 2) Costs to operate a detached dwelling.
> 3) Close proximity to services.
> 4) Climate and accessibility to the outdoors.

Our data showed these factors were the most important considerations for retirees. Earlier, I discussed the advent of stress and its impact on the physiological system of the individual. Seniors need to be stress free during their retirement years. Seniors will spend many hours in their residence once they leave the workplace. The place they chose to live should provide the ambience required to make their life stress free and enjoyable.

Location of Housing and Proximity to Family and Friends:
Location of a senior person's residence is necessary for emotional and physical health. Seniors need to stay in contact with their offspring and friends especially where good relationships have been established. Humans are programmed to be sociable. Bonding commences at childhood and continues throughout one's life. For those who have had good family bonding, sense of well-being, identity, and support from others, there is a need to retain a social network during retirement. This fosters stable emotional well-being and good social relationships.

It is important for seniors to maintain a residence in close proximity to facilities which have become part of one's life style. If the senior wants to have contact with their friends and peers then they need to retire in a central location. This will allow them to also participate in activities similar to those prior to retirement.

Research with humans would indicate that contact comfort is at the basis of good social relationships. When primates or human infants are frightened they seek out solace from a parent figure. In retirement years, older seniors become more dependent on their offspring. They seek support for a variety of activities including shopping, travelling, visiting relatives and in decision making. Good relationships between parent and child during the formative years, sets the stage for good contact and support in later life.

Humans strive for relationships in which they will receive support. People who are emotionally stabile appear to have had biological, adoptive or surrogate parents who were supportive. Emotionally healthy people have been nurtured in a caring environment. The nurturance bestowed upon the child leads to a sense of independence, and emotional stability. This creates a need to be with friends and family members. Stable family environments include nuclear and extended family settings which provide for positive growth. During family gatherings the extended members share in their experience. Family members reconnect and discuss personal issues which are important in their relationships. Discussions between members create a sense of meaningfulness for the individual. Personal contact with family members allows for emotional bonding and a tangible basis for existence. Emotional well-being provides one with the encouragement to go forward with one's life.

Some families have problematic relationships which lead to instability. Feelings of estrangement and social isolation are often evident. Friction in family relationships, leads one to seek out friends for nurturance and support. Friendships much like family relationships provide the individual with a source of contact which can assist with personal development. Supportive friends assist in providing one with the emotional and social resources. These fabricate a sense of well-being.

When one evaluates seniors of the 2000's, there is a need to equate stability, connectedness to family and friendships as important variables in emotional adjustment. Many seniors dream of residing on remote tropical islands and living their final days combing beaches, and walking in serene settings. In fantasy this is a positive reflection, but in reality many seniors want contact with their families. Limited contact with family and friends sometimes creates a state of anxiety, despondency or emotional upheaval in the senior person's life.

Research by Valliant and Furac noted that seniors who resided in northern Ontario, had a need to interact with family, siblings, friends, and children. This was an important variable for well-being during later years. Stability was also enhanced if one owned their own vehicle. This allowed the senior to have interaction with members of their social group especially family and friends. When one explores the issue of retirement residency, seniors admit their intention is to take up residence in a community which provides them with close access to their children. Seniors have more flexibility in their schedules because many do not work after retirement.

They have the time and the means to visit their families, relatives and friends. Being able to access their social contacts enhances their contentment during the senior years.

During my vacations, I have encountered many seniors. Most are receptive and willingly engage in conversations about their lifestyles. These seniors indicate they like to travel but their escapes are short in duration. They return to their homes so they can re-establish contact with families and friends. Needless to say, some seniors who reside in the northern hemisphere travel during winter months when the daylight hours decrease and the north grows colder. Travel to the southern hemisphere ensures a period of time where seniors can engage in outdoor activities in a warm and sunny climate. After 2 to 6 months in these warmer climates, they are ready to return to their permanent residences to re-initiate social and emotional contact with family and friends. Humans are social organisms and need contact with others to provide them with emotional comfort. When seniors are not with family members, they willingly engage in discussion of family related issues. This form of reminiscing provides the senior with emotional security, knowing that in time they will re-unite with family members.

One elderly man informed me that he had always dreamed about moving to the west coast of Canada when he retired. Upon retirement, he immediately packed his household and moved to Vancouver Island. It was his impression that it would be easier adjusting to a temperate climate with predicable weather. After his re-location to Vancouver Island, he found the climate agreed with him. He developed physical stamina and commenced taking care of a large property which had flowers, vegetables, and fruit trees. He resided on Vancouver Island for a decade but eventually came to the recognition that something was missing from his life. The distance from Ontario and the expense for his relatives to visit him made it almost impossible for regular contact. He and his wife longed interaction with family members but could not travel to visit relatives because of their limited pension funds. After 15 years on Vancouver Island, he decided to sell his retirement home. Shortly thereafter, he returned to Ontario so that he could be with his family before he died.

Life has many important lessons. One of these includes the notion of emotional and social bonding. People have a difficult time separating themselves from family members over extended periods. Human contact allows for bonding and this assists in creating emotional stability. Seniors do best during their retirement if they can maintain contact with family members.

Costs to Operate a Detached Dwelling:
Most seniors can only afford one primary residence. This dwelling might not be in close proximity to family members but access can be obtained by a vehicle or public transportation. Seniors generally chose a dwelling which will allow them good access to family and friends. One's dwelling can take the form of a single detached home but in many circumstances it may be a condo or apartment. Research that I conducted with a colleague some years ago showed that emotional health of seniors who resided in detached homes was no different than those who reside in multi-unit apartment buildings. If seniors have physical health and finances to take care of a detached home, they usually preferred this

arrangement. The costs to maintain the dwelling however seemed to play a large factor in the choice of dwelling chosen during retirement years.

Seniors who reside in their own homes generally have disposable income. This allows them to undertake maintenance and upkeep of their homes. Seniors do not get many financial breaks when they retire. If they have not saved adequate money during their working years, the costs to undertake retirement generally places a financial strain on them. With a modest retirement income, many seniors who have paid off their mortgage can afford the expenses necessary for the upkeep of their homes. To some seniors however, this could lead to personal sacrifices. Ownership of a home is an expensive undertaking. It requires considerable money to maintain a home. Government grants are sometimes made available to seniors so they can maintain their homes. Only when the senior can no longer perform maintenance does the single dwelling residence become problematic. Often seniors who can afford to hire outside help to assist with snow removal, grass cutting, raking of leaves and cleaning of exterior windows generally prefer to reside in their homes. When the senior person can no longer do these things, then there is a need for re-consideration of their residence.

Close Proximity to Services:
Some researchers have found that seniors experience greater satisfaction in their lives when their dwelling allows access to community resources. I conducted some research which evaluated distance to specific services (doctor, pharmacy, and grocery store). The data showed that seniors who resided

in close proximity to these services had better emotional stability. In northern Ontario the distance which one must travel to many services can be extreme. Public transportation does not always provide quick access to these services. Seniors who do not have vehicles, or access to public transportation often prefer to reside in multi-unit complexes which have these services available on the premises.

Climate and Accessibility to the Outdoors:
The geographic location which one inhabits can affect mental health of retirees? The mass exodus of retirees to the southern hemisphere during winter months assures us that the weather in the north is not desirable. Many retirees from Canada and the Northern States flock to Florida, Texas and Arizona to escape cold winters. Some research has shown that retirees who spend their winters in the southern climate have elevated emotional satisfaction. They have better access to activities and spend more time in the sun. Those with a propensity toward seasonal affective disorder experience immediate relief because the sun tends to activate the brain neurochemistry and improve mood.

Retirement Communities:
Some people prefer to reside within the community in which they raised their children whereas others prefer to re-locate to retirement communities. There is no easy answer regarding the type of residence which is best suited for seniors. Sociable people like to interact with others who enjoy similar activities. The retiree must make a decision which includes their

interests and needs. Some seniors prefer the home town in which they have resided for most of their working lives. This allows them to interact with people who are part of their social network.

The decision to re-locate to another locale is highly determined by ones' interests or activities. Seniors who enjoy golfing, skiing, biking or walking will generally choose a geographical area which can meet their needs. With retirement comes a change in financial status and this usually predicts where a person decides to reside. There are many retirement communities throughout North America but many seniors cannot afford these lifestyles. It is generally one's economic means which lead to one's residence option. Seniors who have adequate finances, will reside in a setting which suits their lifestyle.

There are many varied regions in North American. These places have much to offer the senior. The area that one chooses to reside will greatly determine their style of living. If the senior loses interest in an area, they can pack their belongings and move to another locale. During my professional career, I met many people who had personal aspirations. They fulfilled these during their working lives but upon retirement made choices to reside in a location best suited to meet their needs and interests. A psychiatrist with whom I had worked during my early career had an interesting approach toward retirement. He had been married for some years and raised three offspring. When I met Frank, he was 48 years of age. His philosophy toward life was rooted in the notion that a frequent change in residence was good for emotional well-being. Furthermore, he believed that it was beneficial for a person to experience different areas of the country.

Consequently, he only remained at a job for a maximum of 5 years and then re-located to another area of the country. Frank believed that his versatile living style would allow him to sample many regions and meet new people. When he was ready to retire, it was his belief that he could reflect on his experiences and return to the region which he believed would offer him the lifestyle that he wanted.

Frank's method of evaluating residential living was interesting, because most people are bound by the confines of their family relationships and jobs. These often restrict one to a particular style of life and lead to a sedentary arrangement in habits. By the time retirement comes, many seniors are steadfast in their social networks replete with family, friends and acquaintances. They do not have any inclination of leaving their domicile in which they reside.

Humans are creatures of habit and predicable in behaviour. They plan their lives and make decisions. The human species isn't so different in behaviours but their cognitive and personality styles have an effect on the way they make decisions. This allows one to make choices regarding lifestyle, friendships and places where they want to reside. Many people are bound by their occupation and the availability of jobs. Others choose employment based upon interests and ability to engage in their personal and recreational activities. Some people "live to work whereas others work to live".

Every region of Canada and the United States has something to offer seniors. The diversity of one's residential location will provide one with a lifestyle based on their particular needs. One of the best ways of making a choice for residential location during retirement is to travel across the country and evaluate the provinces, territories and states.

Many seniors are driven by a need to explore and this allows them to choose their final destiny. Commitment to family and friends will drive some people to remain in the same locale for the greater period of their life. These people are bound by tradition and family relationships.

CHAPTER NINE

AGING ALONE OR WITH OTHERS

Rule #11: People need time alone and time with others.

Humans have a need to associate with others. Interaction with others, allows for social structure, support and safety. As members of a group, people utilize social rules to ensure they are fitting in with other members. Social comparison becomes one of the key factors which allow humans to gauge their activity. When humans are given the choice of selecting to be on their own or to be with others, social psychologists have found most people would rather be with others. This form of behaviour is consistent with basis of social interaction and bonding.

As seniors age, some report their greatest fear is aging alone. Being involved in dyadic relationship allows the senior to share information and be part of a group process. As offspring leave the home, parents are left feeling somewhat isolated and alone. When seniors age and lose their spouses through separation, divorce or death they report feeling lonely. Social isolation and loneliness are commonly found in older people especially as their social circles decrease. Friendships generally allow some compensation for this loss, but as friends die off, seniors face the despair of loneliness. Ross Peters conducted research on loneliness in older people in the last decade. His research showed that 45% of participants over the age of 72 had high levels of loneliness. Furthermore, loneliness seemed to be more prevalent amongst those people who had been widowed less than five years. Apparently, seniors who resided in nursing homes were lonelier than those who did not reside in a nursing home. Louise Hawkley and her colleagues have found that social isolation increases health risks in the elderly. Allan Schwartz found that loneliness which is defined as having no friends or companionship, being solitary, or not having caring family, leads to a plethora of diseases. Being alone during the senior years creates an inordinate amount of stress and innervates the immune response. Long term social isolation and loneliness generally lead to an early demise.

What does it take to decrease loneliness and social isolation in seniors? I have talked to many people beyond the age of 50. From what I have gathered, healthy aging is not garnered from wealth but from contact with others as one becomes disengaged from their jobs. The state of one's mind and attitude appear to be important variables. These coupled with friendships, physical exercise and social activities, are instrumental for successful aging.

In order to achieve longevity and not be afflicted by feelings of isolation and loneliness, seniors need to arrive at senescence content with their earlier lives. People who reach centenarian status generally have had many factors stacked in their favour. These include a sound genetic pool, daily exercise programs, healthy diet and lowered levels of stress in later years. For many centenarians, these factors will allow for increased longevity. On October 21, 2010 I was perusing a National Paper and an article caught my attention. According to the author, two hundred Japanese centenarians had gone missing with no account of their current residential location. These seniors had been residing with relatives but subsequently disappeared. This caused some alarm for the government officials who immediately commenced a search for these missing persons. Forensic evaluation of this matter indicated that some of the centenarians thought to have been living, had in fact already been dead. Ostensibly, one man having achieved the age of 111 years was visited by government officials. They wanted to congratulate him on his birthday and long life status. When this elderly gentleman could not be located a detailed search found that he had been dead for 30 years; his mummified body still remained in his death bed. Apparently, his 81 year old daughter had left him in his bed so that she could collect the deceased man's pension. It is situations such as these which lead us to believe that statistics collected on longevity are not always reliable.

Many have sought the fountain of youth, but none as far as I know have found it. Many seniors seek a style of life which ensures healthy choices which allow for a more productive quality of life. Many have used diet and exercise as the starting point whereas others have focused on contact with family and friends as a way of increasing longevity. Numerous activities and events are used by seniors to make their life more fulfilling. Many seniors have taken an approach which has inspired them to achieve physical, emotional and spiritual success. People are unique, yet different from one another in many ways. The experiences they savour at the fountain of youth are varied. Personality differences motivate and challenge seniors to achieve a level of satisfaction from their lives. The examples that I have provided throughout this book indicate there are many differences amongst seniors and these differences create their identities. Many seniors I have interviewed express a zest for life and appear to live each day for what it provides. Many seniors report having experienced a variety of hurdles in their lives. They had to be resilient in order to cope with these debilitating events during their lifetime.

Many seniors will achieve 80 years of longevity over their life span and some will achieve centenarian status. Life consists of approximately 700 thousand hours, during this time many events take place. The achievements over this period will vary. Some people will accomplish much whereas others will leave no trace of their journey. Some seniors live each day to its fullest. From their inception date and over the course of early childhood, they will endure many experiences. With the onset of adolescence, one's life evolves to include friendships and interaction with peers. Graduation to young adulthood allows one's life to become enmeshed in permanent relationships. Many people achieve significant professional accomplishments over the course of their lives, whereas others foster solid relationships with their family. Some however, lose focus of their lives and don't begin to live until sometime after the age of retirement. They have become too enmeshed in their daily experiences.

The point which I would like to make here is that one has to make the time to experience life to its fullest. In his book "Aging Well", George Vaillant and his co-researchers interviewed many people over their life. Some people who were initially miserable, or had desperate life stories regardless of their professional status, were just as miserable when they were later interviewed in life. These desperate people or what Vaillant termed the "sad-sick" never achieved contentment with their life. Their "miserable status" appeared to have been caused by their poor attitude toward life; their lifestyle arose from this "inner negativity". In today's society, people who procure a "miserable status" need to seek out therapy so they can cope with their existence. Therapists can provide some insight. Through conventional avenues, including cognitive and behavioral therapies the "sad sick" can begin to understand their underlying problems. This could be of value in fostering personal change in attitude and enable them to have a better life. Without an exploration of underlying issues, seniors could remain members of a "sad-sick group", never capable of evolving to a higher level of well-being. They will never achieve contentment in their lives.

During senior years, there will be time for reflection on one's life. Seniors build memories through life's experiences. There is nothing more despairing for the aging senior than to realize their lives have been meaningless. It is better to have loved, than to never have ventured into the realm of love. Seniors need to be wanted and need to be part of something no matter how small. Loneliness is merely the recognition that one has failed by not developing long lasting relationships.

CHAPTER 10

FINAL PASSAGE

Rule #12: Life has a beginning and an end.

As one approaches the final stage of life, the search for meaning becomes an important pursuit. Seniors often ponder whether they should merely enjoy each day as it unfolds or make detailed plans to accommodate their lifestyle. Reflecting on their past lives, elderly people question whether their lives have been of value. Relationships have evolved from the birth and nurturing of their offspring. Parents bond with their children and develop relationships. Others have developed an attachment to the working world through their professions.

The twenty first century will be an important time for many. During this period, events will unfold and have an impact on the lives of many. Environmental events including changes in the ozone layers over the poles, climatic warming and global catastrophes will have some effect on our lives. Many wonder whether they should fear these events or merely use these to understand the meaning of existence.

There have been many transitions from the time

of early hominids. Neanderthal and Cro-Magnon man no longer exist, but Homo sapiens have continued to evolve to their present stage. The Genome Project has provided evidence that humans commenced their inception in Central Africa and then migrated to geographical locations over the past millennium. One can only wonder whether evolution occurred linearly or was the result of a logarithmic explosion. The Genome project has shown that a small percentage of DNA crossed from the Neanderthal population to our present Homo sapien lineage.

Today, scientists continue to manipulate DNA with the impression this will somehow benefit society. Recently, I read in the Globe and Mail of experimentation which has allowed scientists to increase the weight of fish in a ten fold direction. The benefit according to these scientists would lead to larger fish which could be used to feed the hungry populace. Many geneticists are concerned with the manipulation of nature because of the possible impact that consumption of hybrid forms could have on human genes.

From the year 5000 B.C. to 1800 A.D. there was little advancement in science. With Alexander Graham Bell's discovery of communication via the telephone and Guglielmo Marconi's advancement of the wireless radio, a new era was upon us. With the transition to the 2000's, satellite technology has created ways of communicating that one could never have imagined. Telecommunications over the past 100 years has had a significant impact on the way we transfer information. Computer technology, and other more recent scientific advancements have evolved in such a manner that society is now in a state of flux.

This transition should spark our interest in the

meaning of existence. Where do we come from and where do we go? Is there a higher power or should one simply deduce that we have evolved from the amoeba and will simply undergo physical transitions as the future expands. Book stores and the World Wide Web are replete with educational material espousing scientific ideology, spirituality, and new age specialties. This new wave of existentialism has many of us thinking. Those who seem most interested in these concepts appear to be the post war baby boomers. Many have attempted to evaluate their roots and re-establish ties with the new age phenomenon as a way of coping with their renewed consciousness. Others have merely attempted to understand their existence.

Why are people searching for meaning to explain their existence during this era? The twentieth century brought forth more time for leisure and recreation. People work less and subsequently have more time on their hands to explore their beliefs regarding the universe. Even those who cannot find the time to browse through library collections have found ways of accessing information from media sources. Like the early philosophers, many have immersed themselves in the literature and used this information to take control of their lives. Most humans want control and predictability of their lives. This is observed in procreation choices, including gender of child, and the elimination of defective genes. No one is willing to allow nature to take its course. This need for control motivates people to accept responsibility for their destiny. If there is a higher power capable of providing salvation, seniors appear driven to achieve the ultimate experience. The search for meaning expands one's need for an understanding of the afterlife.

Research has shown that having some belief in a higher power appear to make seniors happier and more accepting of aging and death. Does religiosity, new wave spirituality, or cosmic consciousness act as a driving force in one's search for meaning? Does humanity have a need for a destiny? Most would agree that to be human is to express an interest in a past, present and future. Conditioning from the time one was a youngster has played a pivotal role in this integral pursuit. Today's generation are a unique group in that they are filled with needs. Their position in the time spectrum makes them a malleable group but at the same time creates delusions of entitlement.

Those raised in North America at the turn of the 19th century were filled with ideals. People worked six days a week, attended church on Sunday and spent the remainder of the day with their family. Children were raised with values. With the economic disaster of the 1920's and 1930's, mind sets were altered. Children raised during this period came to understand that work would not always be available. Consequently, from an early age they realized their wishes may not reach fruition. Expectancies during this period brought about different thinking patterns. People began to realize that to adapt, one had to have flexible thinking. As seniors emerged from the Great Depression and World War Two, they did not ask "how do I retire successfully"? They merely accepted their position in life, knowing they had made it through a volatile period of history. The generation of post war baby boomers that appeared a generation later are different from those who made it out of this tumultuous era.

The greatest hurdle people face today is whether they will retain their job and have sufficient funds to retire.

Also of concern is the economic future of their children. Will they be able to afford higher education for their offspring? Will their children have the ability to secure future employment? Baby boomers are undergoing a massive restructuring in their thinking because of forced economic times. They are reflecting on information and asking questions about their existence because of the realities of this time period. Their concern for the future sometimes borders on angst. In response, they have sought answers. Solace seems to be obtained collectively through "group talk". Psychologists refer to this behaviour as social comparison. This includes sharing information with friends and acquaintances. In this manner, they attempt to ensure they have similarity in thoughts and behaviour to other members of the populace. In the process of "group talk" they have been re-introduced to old values and new ideals. The quest for meaning in life becomes important because of their concern for the future. As a way of coping with their dilemmas, some become optimists whereas others become pessimists. Orientation in behaviour is toward a value which they can comprehend.

One can only ask whether there are benefits gained from the search to explain existence? Does religion, new age spiritualism or cosmic consciousness calm the masses? Does it provide the answers and serve as the fountain of youth for the aged? Does it give seniors renewed energy to assist in new future directions? Do the spiritually inclined have fewer fears and anxieties regarding their destiny? Ann Downey maintains that fear is a state of mind which many encounter during old age as they prepare for death. Three types of individuals emerged from her research on death: 1) some admit to the fear of death; 2) some claim indifference toward death;

and 3) some welcome death.

There are many individual reactions to fear. Some authors argue that those with stronger religious values tend to have less fear of death, especially if they believe there is another plain of existence after death. Research by Herman Feifel and Vivian Nagy has shown that individuals with high fear of death were in fact less religious than others. Research by Ann Downey has found that contrary to what some have said, religion did not reduce fear of death in middle age professional males with a mean age of 48.2 years. Other researchers do not support her findings because they believe that religious attitude can vary for many. For example, Michael Leming believes that it isn't so much one's religious attitude but the strength of one's religious commitment which can explain fear of death. Those who are strongly committed to their religious values do not question death in their final phase, because in their mind they are convinced that a "supreme being" will provide for their journey. Some people believe they will be rewarded with everlasting existence.

My study of Eastern and Western religions has left me with the understanding that regardless of focus, many people believe in a supreme deity who will provide a transition to a higher level of existence. For example, Norman Vincent Peale in his book entitled "The Power of Positive Thinking" believes that only a true creator can assist with the final passage. There are many different perspectives which one can adhere to in their beliefs regarding religion. Some believe in oneness with the universe whereas others advocate a back to basics philosophy through spiritual guidance. Seniors that I have interviewed do not look forward to death. They believe that medical science has promised them a specified period of longevity. Death is not appealing to able bodied, emotionally and mentally stable people.

Medical science has advanced the notion, that humans in North America can live approximately 80 years; with women on the average living longer than men. Statistics Canada research has shown that women's average life expectancy is about 83 whereas men will live until approximately 79 years. Whether we reach our average life expectancy or expire ahead of time is an unknown. Every day that one exists beyond the expected age, is an added bonus. The length of one's life, is dependent upon many factors including genetics, diet, exercise, lifestyle, stress, and disease.

New age gurus advocate that one can tap into consciousness or some cosmic clock and this will slow the aging process. This is an interesting assumption but like Greek mythology, soothsayers are merely attempting to numb our senses to the fact that we must die. With their new found ideologies "New Age Gurus" are merely trying to insulate us from our inevitable fate. Death has become a taboo word because most people fear death. Those who have had near death experiences following accident, ill health or injury and having recovered, show an elevated level of fear following their discharge from hospital. The omnipresent emotion of fear emerges as the true master of these patients. According to some, fear becomes the pervasive feeling after death experiences. Some believe this is due to an overwhelming emotional response, whereas others believe this occurs because some people have no faith or belief in a higher power.

What should be the focus of one's life? Should one espouse hedonistic views or worry about tomorrow? Baby boomers comprise a large percentage of the population in the

Western world. In their quest for answers, they seek meaning to explain their existence. They were raised to believe that work was a means to an end. By working diligently one was assured a comfortable existence with all the trappings of middle class values. Many baby boomers between 50 and 65 years of age have realized their material dreams. They have accomplished the ideals which they had fantasized about during their adolescent years. They have acquired their middle class values. They have raised children, realized a healthy life and now have a comfortable retirement. Their focus is now to sip at the fountain of youth. New fad diets, vitamins, cosmetics and surgery are sought in their pursuit for the good life. Ponce de Leon searched for that fountain of youth and never found it. Much like the early explorers, baby boomers quest for longevity is equally nebulous. Spirituality promises everything and establishes a new hope. For others spirituality promises nothing. A quick fix is sought and many grasp for it. But this only serves as a temporary crutch, and like most prosthetic devices may not sustain or prolong life.

Western society is a plastic cosmopolitan. Baby boomers have been raised to consume and discard goods. Fashionable items are created only to become replaceable commodities. This satisfies consumer mentality conditioned by our Western values. Norman Vincent Peale stated that humans need to become acquainted with a higher power. In today's society, Peale's teachings seem to have taken a back burner. In many parts of the USA, especially the Baptist Belt however, Peale's ideals still pack some punch having become an elixir to sedate the masses. In his book, "The God Delusion", Richard Dawkins has expanded on the earlier ideas presented in Michael Persinger's book, "The Neuropsychological Bases of God". Persinger's work maintains the thesis that "god is nothing but a mythical being" created to placate the anxiety of the masses.

Many seniors attempt to come to terms with their fear of death. Many choose religion to assist in this endeavour, whereas others use the classical defense mechanisms of repression and rationalization. They chose to consciously forget about death or rationalize the concept. During their working lives, many people are too busy to reflect on the concept of death. Once they become disengaged from the workforce, they begin to evaluate the transition to death, the next stage of their life. They not only seek comfort in recognizing that life is not infinite but must cope with the thought of loss of family and friends once they reach this final phase.

Successful aging does require an inherent need for meaning or an understanding of the balance of life and death. Victor Frankl discussed the importance of a search for meaning. His early life in Nazi concentration camps convinced him one had to focus on every day lived, and not the past or the future. Erik Erikson noted that by the time one has achieved old age, he or she will have recognized whether they have accomplished a sense of integrity. This will only prevail if the senior has achieved some importance from their life. Those who have not found relevance from their existence, become despairing and miserable. As one's health begins to fail in old age, a sense of hope for the future must be established. If that hope can be garnered from spirituality, then seniors become assured of an afterlife. Religion and new age philosophies sit well with seniors who have a sense of hope because it thrusts them into the realm of cosmic spirituality. This provides for an acceptance of the aging process and allows the senior to believe they will become one with the universe.

In the 1970's, scientists advocated the importance of taking charge of the aging process. According to research, this could be done by becoming socially and mentally engaged during the retirement years. In the 1980's, there was a shift in thinking which advocated that to age well one had to become involved in exercises. One's health could also be improved through the use of proper diet. These in combination would become the elixir to longevity. Today modern science has encouraged a new thinking toward successful aging which includes balancing natural nutrient intake with reasonable levels of exercise.

Successful aging can be obtained through proactive thinking and planning. Seniors have to become introspective about their lives. They must seek solutions to myriad events they encounter. In the event seniors do not have the answers they can consult experts. Physicians trained in health medicine can evaluate the senior person's physical health and diet. Conversely, psychologists can evaluate behavioral and cognitive strategies. Internal mechanisms which drive and motivate behaviour have to be evaluated.

In my clinical work with depressed patients, I have learned the root for suicide seems to exist when one looses their interest in the pursuit of future goals. Victor Frankl created logotherapy to assist patients in their search for meaning. Frankl believed that humans require a will to enhance their existence. Some advocate a hedonistic approach toward life as noted in the dictum "live for today for tomorrow you may die". Others however strive to tap into "a higher plane of consciousness" and somehow become one with the universe.

Through religion and its spiritual underpinnings one attempts to achieve their final destiny. With the meaning of life explained, it is easier to undertake the human journey. Death is not finite but only a transition to a better future. Most humans do not like to perceive themselves as highly metamorphosized amoebas. Scientists have scrutinized religious behaviour in their attempt to provide answers to this debate. As health fails in the senior citizen, they are forced to reminisce about their past and their future. Many prefer to focus on their past because the future seems bleak. Others who have visualized spirituality and a conviction to a higher power, believe greater rewards will follow after their death. The transition to a higher plane becomes a fruitful and omnipresent view.

In our modern society, we have begun to counsel people to view old age with intrepidation. In the event the senior becomes a burden because of illness or disease, one is taught to consider alternatives including euthanasia. The balance of life must be consistent with prescribed conditions. When life is no longer purposeful, we teach the elderly to avoid and escape it. The teachings of euthanasia are entirely in contradiction to spiritual and religious teachings. Thomas Cole believes that euthanasia is a naive teaching as its premise is based on intellect and science and not in line with religious ideals. Research by Paul Wong has shown that an aging person's search for meaning is complemented, when society includes; 1) dignity and value in spite of illness and frailty, and 2) assists the aged individual via social support systems by caring for spiritual well-being and re-affirming the positive role of old age. Paul Wong maintained that agencies have been created to assist aged populations with their physical, social and economic needs during their final stage of existence.

For seniors, one of the most important needs is to understand the meaning of life. Without purpose, humans don't function well and according to psychologists develop a state of helplessness and depression. Matilda Riley and Anne Foner have found that men and women in their 60's have a high level of church attendance but this drops off with advanced age. The factors responsible include, physical inability to attend church, lack of transportation and / or infirm mental and emotional health. A study by Kyriakos Markides and his colleagues showed that religious values were a significant predictor of life satisfaction. Others including Dan Blazer and Erdman Palmore have evaluated the elderly in a longitudinal study. They found that women were more religious in their attitudes than men. Furthermore, people who worked in non-manual professions had a higher level of religiosity than those involved in manual professions. From their research, it became evident that positive religious attitudes remained stable over an 18 year period. There have been a number of studies which have discussed the positive impact of attending church on one's attitude, life satisfaction, feelings of well-being and adaptation to old age. Information available shows that in the aged population (ie. people between the ages of 80 to 100) there is a greater likelihood to use religion as a coping mechanism. Humans find support, comfort and hope in their religious values.

Statistics Canada has made it clear that the average age expectancy is approximately 80 years. As seniors reach this age, they become more cognizant of their imminent death. By the time most seniors have achieved old age, they have experienced a critical incident in their life. Whether it is personal illness, or the loss of loved ones, seniors begin to understand that death is inevitable. One must cherish each moment they are alive and live it to the fullest. Each breath that is inhaled into one's lungs is more powerful than all the elixirs that can be purchased in a health food store or pharmacy.

Aging should not represent a negative experience but one with a positive ending. The closer one moves toward death, the shorter the distance to a state of peacefulness. Death should not be viewed as the final stage of our metamorphosis but the frontier between the tangible and the spiritual self.

EPILOGUE

NANOTECHNOLOGY: A NEW MILLENNIUM

Statistics Canada has provided us with the numbers. In our present day society, one can be assured that with good genetics, exercise and a healthy diet it is easy to achieve the age of 80. Within the next century this will likely expand to the age of 100. By 2100, there should be many centenarians existing on this planet. However, many wonder about the not so distant future? What can one expect from scientific investigations currently underway? Will scientists fabricate an elixir to enable one's body increased longevity?

Sometime between 50,000 to 80,000 years ago, the Neanderthals and Cro-Magnons drifted into oblivion. Research has shown modern man possess some genetic material similar to our ancestors. Much like the early plain dwellers who travelled to North America some 7000 years ago, Homo sapiens have flourished because of their development of a language. This has allowed for communication and technical advancement. The human species has been bound by a sense of determinism to fulfil their expectancies. This has lead to the dawn of a new millennium and the search for an elixir which will increase longevity. Cryogenics has already created a need for futuristic "human banks" where people with ailments beyond the scope of modern medicine are having themselves frozen so they can be revived at a later time when medical science has advanced to provide a cure for their ailment.

As one searches for the elixir to slow aging, options will have to be exercised to ameliorate disease which ravage the human body. Licit and illicit drugs have already begun showing up in the marketplace. They will become a venue of choice to decrease the impact of aging. Others will seek advanced medical technology or use genetic engineering to remove defective genes. In some cases, genetic material may be implanted to prolong life. The more adventurous will seek bioengineering and computer technology interfacing as a way of advancing their lives. It would be conceivable to use nanotechnology as a way of adding "new hardware" when the "old hardware" wears out. For the senior whose hippocampus (memory centre) begins to fade with aging, a consideration could be to add an artificial brain implant to compensate for memory loss. By uploading existing memories onto a "nanochip" and re-wiring these to existing brain hardware would allow the senior some restorative function. Neurochips could be installed to void the loss of cerebral function caused by Alzheimer's disease and dementias.

Research by Naweed Syed and his colleagues at the University of Calgary's Hotchkiss Brain Institute has shown that brain cells can be wired to silicon chips. One can envision these microcomputer silicon neurochips as the new wave of nanotechnology. They will provide communication between cells and microcontrollers. A programmed neurochip could replace defective brain structures. This hardware would have the capability of ordering the cell and the brain into action. Nanotechnologists with advanced expertise could insert neurochips into the cerebral cortex to falsely advise the telomeres within the cells they have already divided and therefore not have the need for further cell division. In this way, cell integrity would be assured and the telomeres would not deteriorate leading to aging of cells; inadvertently aging would be placed on hold.

Nanotechnology could become the elixir of the future. Defective cells and brain structures would be replaced through the use of micro-neurochips. These would serve to improve the integrity of the brain-body interactions. Rather than seeking cures for ailments including multiple sclerosis, Alzheimer disease, Parkinson disorder, dementias, and spinal chord damage, micro-neurochips would be installed to enhance neural communication by replacing defective cells and brain structures.

Other uses of neurochips could include those envisioned in the science fiction writing "Nanowired". In this futurist novel, nanotechnology is used to insert neurochips into the brains of offender populations. These assist in re-programming pro-social behaviours in the offender population thereby circumventing criminal sentiments and antisocial behaviour.

There are many benefits which can be derived from the implementation of nanotechnology. Many of these will advance science in a positive direction by making techniques available to the populace. If one can envision these new models implemented to assist with brain dysfunction, the major benefit would be the control of CNS damage. Seniors realize they have a specified amount of time on earth. When some genetic fluke, disease or accident interferes with the 80 years each of us in entitled, then the medical application of nanotechnology would be implemented to thwart the disease process. Toward the end of one's life there will be a number of choices. One can either accept the decrepitude of aging or the implementation of advanced techniques to ensure survival; this will not allow the human journey to falter.

Recently, I perused the January 2010 edition of National Geographic and read an article entitled, "Merging Man and Machine the Bionic Age". The article by Josh Hirschman evaluates the modern age of medicine. Ostensibly mechanical techniques are now being devised to assist people who loose sensory modalities (ie. sight, hearing or limbs). New technologies allow for the bypassing of sensory systems so that information can be re-routed directly to the brain, thereby allowing for perception of a sensory experience. Bioengineering and computer technology have led to Brain Computer Interfacing (BCI). BCI has myriad implications for modern medicine. This technique allows amputees to not only sense but re-direct the motor communication to artificial limbs thereby allowing them to grasp items, walk or run. In 1982, medical experimentation by William DeVries showed that a Jarvik artificial heart could be installed in a patient. In the last thirty years there have been many medical gains since this pioneering work.

Brain computer interfacing coupled with nanotechnology, will expand exponentially to increase life. The twenty-first century will usher in medical accomplishments which will exacerbate a new era. Brain structures which have failed through accident, disease or aging will be replaced.

Parkinson patients will no longer have to worry about ingesting chemical substances to allow for cerebro-motor control. Instead, they will have programmed silicon chips inserted into their basal ganglia. Their sensory and motor functions will be controlled by the programs installed in the neurochips. The future of aging will give rise to a new wave of thinking; one in which aging citizens can assert some control of their destiny. By consenting to the implantation of nanotechnology will allow seniors some advancement in the quality of their life. Medication for ailments will still exist but will only play a small part in treatment. Genetic engineering, brain computer interfacing and nanotechnology could become the new elixir; the fountain of youth.

REFERENCES

Abraham, C. (2010) Calgary Scientists to Create Human Neurochip. Globe Life From Globe and Mail Published August 09, 2010.

Aggarwal, K. (2009) Brain-Computer Interfaces: Blurring the Distinction Between Flesh and Metal. Berkeley Scientific Journal, Technology and Human Interaction, Fall, Vol. 13 (1), 11-13.

Ames, B.N. (2004). Mitochondrial Decay a Major Cause of Aging Can be Delayed. Journal of Alzheimer Disease, Vol. 6 (2), 117-121.

Angier, B. (1978) Field Guide to Medicinal Wild Plants. Stackpole Books, Harrisburg, Pennsylvania.

Aubert, G., Lansdorp, PM. (2008) Telomeres and Aging Physiological Reviews, 88 (2), 557-579.

Baker, L. et. al. (2010) Effects of Aerobic Exercise on Mild Cognitive Impairment. Archives of Neurology, 67 (1), 13-14.

Bandura, A. (1965). Vicarious Processes. A Case of Non-trial Learning. In L. Berkowitz (Ed.), Advances in Experimental Social Psychology. Vol. 2, Academic Press, New York.

Beland, F. (1987). Living Arrangement Preferences Among Elderly People. The Gerontologist, Vol. 27 (6), 797-803.

Birbaumer, N. (2006) Breaking the Silence: Brain-computer Interfaces for communication and motor control. Psychophysiology, 43, 517-532.

Blazer, D.& Palmore, E. (1976) Religion and Aging in A Longitudinal Panel. The Gerontologist 16 (1), 82-85.

Bortz, W.M., & Wallace, D.H. (1999) Physical Fitness, Aging, and Sexuality. Journal of Western Medicine, 170, 167-169.

Botwinick, J. (1977) Intellectual Abilities. In J.E. Birren & K.W. Schaie (Eds.) Handbook of the Psychology of Aging. New York: Van Nostrand Reinhold, 580-605.

Brown, D.R., Yore, M.M., Ham, S.A., Macera, C.A. (2005) Physical Activity Among Adults > 50 years with and without Disabilities. Medicine and Science in Sports and Exercise, 620-629.

Business of Aging: Where to Live When We Get Old. http://blog.seniorcaremarketer.com/business_of_aging/nursing_homes/ August 15, 2010.

Charter, R.A. & Alekoumbides, A. (2004) Evidence for Aging as the Cause of Alzheimer's Disease. Psychological Reports, 95, 935-945.

Chilton, D. (1989) The Wealthy Barber. Stoddart, Toronto.

Chodzko-Zajko, W.J. (1991) Physical Fitness, Cognitive Performance and Aging. Medicine and Science in Sports and Exercise, 23 (3), 868-872.

Chodzko-Zajko, W.J. (1998) Physical Activity and Aging: Implications for Health and Quality of Life in Older Persons. President's Council of Physical Fitness and Sports Research Digest, Series 3 (4).

Clement, B.R. (2010) Supplements Exposed. New Page Books, Franklin Lake, New Jersey.

Cole, T.R. (1984) Aging, Meaning and Well-Being: Musings of a Cultural Historian. International Journal of Aging and Human Development, 19 (4), 329-335.

Colicos, M.A. & Syed, N.I. (2006) Neuronal Networks and Synaptic Plasticity of the Brain: Understanding Complex System Dynamics by Interfacing Neurons with Silicon Technologies. Journal of Experimental Biology, 209, 2312-2319.

Cooperberg, C. (2010) Boomers Put Health at Top of Retirement Priorities. Special to the Globe and Mail, December 17.

Covey, R. (2004) The 7 Habits of Highly Effective People. 15 Edition, Free Press, New York.

Craik, F. & Stuss, D. (2010) Will Brain Fitness Games Help Me Stay Mentally Sharp? Globe and Mail, Tuesday July 13, 2010.

Cravit, D. (2010) Did You Have Your Brain Workout Today. CarpHealth e-Bulletin. www.imakenews.com/carppromotions/e

Dekosky, S. et al. (2008) Ginkgo Biloba for Prevention of Dementia. The Journal of the American Medical Association, Vol. 300, No. 19.

Dekosky, S. et al. (2009) Ginkgo Biloba for Preventing Cognitive Decline in Older Adults. The Journal of the American Medical Association, Vol. 302, No 24.

Dixon, R.A., Rust, T., Feltmate, S., and Kwong See, (2007) Memory and Aging: Selected Research Directions and Application Issues. Canadian Psychology, May, Vol. 48 (2) 67-76.

Dooley, S. & Frankel, G. (1990) Improving Attitudes Toward Elderly Persons: Do Differences Exist. Canadian Journal on Aging. Vol. 9 (4), 400-409.

Doulis, A. (1994) Take your Money and Run. Uphill, Toronto.

Downey, A.M. (1984) Relationship of Religiosity to Death Anxiety of Middle-Aged Males. 54, 811-822.

Duke, J. (2001) Essential Herbs, St. Martins Press, New York.

Dunn, M., Brinton, S., & Clark, L (2010) Universal Sex Differences in Online Advertisers Age Preferences: Comparing Data from 14 Cultures and Two Religious Groups. Journal of Evolution and Behavior, May Edition.

Erber, J.T., Szuchman, L.T. & Rothberg, S.T. (1992) Dimensions of Self-Report About Everyday Memory in Young And Older Adults. International Journal of Aging and Human Development, 43 (4), 311-323.

Erikson, E.H. (1963) Childhood and Society, W.W. Norton, New York.

Feifel, H. & Nagy, V.T. (1981) Another Look At Fear of Death. Journal of Consulting and Clinical Psychology, 49, 278-286.

Fischman, J. (2010) The Bionic Age, Merging Man and Machine, National Geographic, January, Vol. 217, (1).

Fisher, B.J. (1992) Successful Aging and Life Satisfaction Journal of Aging Studies, 6 (2), 191-202.

Frankl, V. (1963) Man's Search for Meaning: An Introduction to Logotherapy. Beacon Press, Boston.

Frikke-Schmidt, R., Norestgaard, B., Thudium, D., Gronholdt, M., Tybjaerg-Hansen, A. (2001) APOE Genotype AD and other Dementia but not Ischemic Cerebrovascular Disease. Neurology, 56, 194-200.

Gold, C.H.. Malmberg, B., McClearn, G., Pedersen, N. & Berg, S. (2002) A Study of Older Unlike Sex Twins. The Journal of Gerontology Series B; Psychological and Social Science, 57, 168-176.

Goodman, L.S. & Gilman, A. (1975) The Pharmacological Basis of Therapeutics. Fifth Edition, MacMillan Publishing Company, New York.

Guy, R.F. (1982) Religion, Physical Disabilities and Life Satisfaction in Older Age Cohorts. International Journal of Aging and Human Development, 15 (3), 225-232.

Graedon, J. & Graedon, T. (1999) The Peoples Pharmacy. Guide to Home and Herbal Remedies. St. Martin's Paperbacks, New York.

Gray, G.R., Ventis, D.G., Hayslip, B. (1992) Socio-Cognitive Skills as a Determinant of Life Satisfaction in Aged Persons. International Journal of Aging and Human Development 35 (3), 205-218.

Haitsma, K.V. (1986) Intrinsic Religious Orientation: Implications in the Study of Religiosity and Personal Adjustment in the Aged. The Journal of Social Psychology, 126 (5), 685-687.

Hawkley, L.C. & Cacioppo, J.T. (2007) Aging and Loneliness. Current Direction in Psychological Science, Vol. 16 (4), 187-191.

Hayflick, L. (1965) The Limited In Vitro Lifetime of Human Diploid Cell Strains. Experimental Cellular Research, 37 (3), 614-636.

Havighurst, R., (1961) Successful Aging. Gerontologist 1, 4-7.

Hawkley, L., Berntson, G., Engeland, G., , Masucha, P. & Cacioppo, J. (2005) Stress, Aging and Resilience: Can Accrued Wear and Tear be Slowed? Canadian Psychology, 96, 115-125.

Higginbottom, S.F., Barling, J. & Kelloway, E.K. (1993) Linking Retirement Experiences and Marital Satisfaction: A Mediational Approach. Psychology and Aging, 8 (4), 508 516.

Holden, K.C. (1993) Continuing Limits on Productive Aging; The Lesser Rewards for Working Women: In Achieving a Productive Aging Society; Editor F.G. Laro and Yung Ping Chen, Auburn. Westport, Conn.

Houx, P.J., & Jolles, J. (1993) Age Related Decline of Psychomotor Speed : Effects of Age, Brain Health, Sex and Education. Perceptual and Motor Skills, 76, 195-221.

Http://jama.ama-assn.org/content/288/14/1728.abstract

Http://jama.ama-assn.org/content/303/3/235.abstract

Http://www.annecollins.com/obesity/statistics-obesity.htm

Http://www.canadianliving.com/health/nutrition/the_best_5antioxidant foods

Http://www.cdc.gov/obesity/data/index.html

Http://www.nationmaster.com/graph/hea_obe-health-obesity

Http://www.ncsl.org/default.aspx?tabid=14367

Http://www.phytochemicals.info

Http://www.usatoday.com/news/health/weightloss/2010-01-13-obesity-rates_N.htm

Hutch, D.F., Hammer, M. & Small, B.J. (1993) Age Differences in Cognitive Performance in Later Life: Relationships to Self-Reported Health and Activity Style. Journal of Gerontology: Psychological Sciences, 48 (1), 1-11.

Keith, P.M. (1988) Finances of Unmarried Elderly People over Time. International Journal of Aging and Human Development, 26 (3), 211-222.

Kingsberg, S.A. (2000) The Psychological Impact of Aging on Sexuality and Relationships. Journal of Women's Health and Gender Based Medicine, 9 (1), 33-38.

Kinsey, A., Pomeroy, W., Martin, C.E. (1948) Sexual Behaviour in the Human Male. Saunders, Philadelphia.

Kinsey, A., Pomeroy, W., Martin, C.E. & Gebhard, P. (1953) Sexual Behavior in the Human Female. Saunders, Philadelphia.

Krause, N., Nelson, J., Rock, K. (2008) Financial Strain, Negative Social Interaction and Self-rated Health: Evidence from Two USA Nationwide Longitudinal Surveys, Ageing and Society, 28, 1001-1023.

Kubler-Ross, E. (1969) On Death and Dying. MacMillan, New York.

Laurin, D., Perrault, R., Lindsay, J., Macpherson, K., and Rockwood, K. (2001) Physical Activity and Risk of Cognitive Impairment and Dementia in Elderly Persons. Archives of Neurology, 58 (3), 498-504.

Leaf, A. & Launois, J. (1973) Every Day is a Gift When You are Over 100. National Geographic, Vol. 143 (1), 93-118.

Levy, J. (1994) Impotence and its Medical and Psychosocial Correlates: Results of the Massachusetts Male Aging Study. Journal of Urology, 151, 54-61.

Lemming, M.R. (1979) Religion and Death: A Test of Homans Thesis. Omega, 10, 347-363.

Lewin, K. (1935) A Dynamic Theory of Personality. McGraw-Hill, New York.

Liu, J., Ataman, H., Kristine, H., & Ames, B.N. (2002) Delaying Brain Mitochondrial Decay and Aging with Mitochondrial Antioxidants and Metabolites. Annals of New York Academy of Sciences, Vol. 959, 136-166.

Logue, B.J. (1991) Women at Risk: Predictors of Financial Stress for Retired Women Workers. The Gerontologist 31 (5), 657-665.

Lorenz, K. (1950) The Comparative Method in Studying Innate Behavior Patterns. Symposium of Social Experimental Biology, Animal Behaviour, 4, 221-268, Cambridge.

Markides, K.S.(1983) Aging, Religiosity and Adjustment: A Longitudinal Analysis, Journal of Gerontology, Vol. 38(5)621-625.

Maslow, A. (1961) Toward A Psychology of Being. Van Nostrand, Princeton, NJ.

Maslow, A. (1956) Personality Problems and Personality Growth. In C.G. Moustakas (Ed.). The Self: Explorations in Personal Growth. 232-256, Harper, New York.

Masters, W.H. & Johnson, V.E. (1966) Human Sexual Response. Bantam Books, New York.

McConnell, J.V.(1962) Memory Transfer Through Cannibalism in Planarians. Journal of Neuropsychiatry 3, Monograph Supplement.

Mendes, De Leon, C.F. (1994) Financial Strain and Symptoms of Depression in a Community Sample of Elderly Men and Women. Journal of Aging and Health, Vol. 6 (4), 448-468.

Meston, C.M. (1997) Aging and Sexuality. Western Journal of Medicine, 167 (4), 285-290.

Meston, C.M. & Heiman, J. (1998) Ephedrine-Activated Physiological Sexual Activity in Women. Archives of General Psychiatry, Vol.5 (7).

Mor-Barak, M.E., Scharlach, A.E.,Birba, L., & Sokolov, J. (1992) Employment, Social Networks and Health in The Retirement Years. International Journal of Aging and Human Development, 35 (2), 145-159.

Morley, J. E. (2006) Sexuality and Aging in Principles and Practice of Geriatric Medicine, 4th Edition, Edited by M.S. John Pathy and Alan J.E. Morley, John Wiley and Sons, New York.

Morley, J.E., & Tariq, S.H. (2003) Sexuality and Disease. Clinics in Geriatric Medicine, 19, 563-573.

Mulligan, C. (2010) Seniors Health Requires Multi-Faceted Approach. The Sudbury Star, September 30 Issue, 3.

Murphy, D., Daneman, M., Schneider, A. (2006) Why Do Older Adults Have Difficulty Following Conversations? Psychology and Aging,21, (1), 49-61.

Myerson, J., Hale, S., Wagstaff, D., Poon, L.W., Smith, G.A. (1990) The Information Loss Model: A Mathematical Theory of Age-Related Cognitive Slowing. Psychological Review, 97 (4), 475-487.

National Post (2010) Japan Loses Track of Nearly 200 Centenarians, August 12 Edition.

Neugarten, B.L.(1977) Personality and aging. In J.E. Birren & K.W. Schaie (eds.) Handbook of Psychology and Aging. Van Nostrand Reinhold, 626-649, New York.

Newbern, V.B. (1992) Sharing the Memories: The Value of Reminiscence as a Research Tool. Journal of Gerontological Nursing 18 (5), 13-18.

Nkongolo, K. (2011) The Genetics of Aging. Personal Communication, Biology Department, Laurentian University.

Nussbaum, M.R., Singh A.R., & Pyles, A.A. (2004) Sexual Healthcare Needs of Women Aged 65 and Older. Journal of the American Geriatrics Society, 20, 607-617.

Palmore, E. (1979) Predictors of Successful Aging. The Gerontologist 19 (5), 427-431.

Park, D. & Reuter-Lorenz, P. (2009) The Adaptive Brain. Aging and Neurocognitive Scaffolding. Annual Review of Psychology, Vol. 60, 173-196.

Pate, R., O'Neill, J., Lobelo, F. (2008) The Evolving Definition of Sedentary. Exercise and Sport Science Reviews, 36 (4),173-178.

Peale, N.V. (1956) The Power of Positive Thinking. Fawcett Crest, New York.

Peters,R. (2004) Social Isolation and Loneliness, Centre on Aging. www.coag.uvic.ca/documents/research

Reker, G.T., Peacock, E.J., & .Wong, P.T. (1987) Meaning and Purpose in Life and Well Being: A Life Perspective. Journal of Gerontology 42 (1), 44-49.

Riley, M.W. & Foner.A (1968) Aging and Society. Russell Sage, New York.

Roos, N. & Roos, L. (2002) Surgical Rate Variations: Do They Reflect the Health of Socioeconomic Characteristics of the Population. Medical Care, Vol. 20 (9), 945.

Roozendaal, B. & de Quervain, D.F.J. (2005) Glucocorticoid Therapy and Memory Function. Lessons Learned from Basic Research. Neurology, Vol. 64, (2) 184-185.

Ryff, C.D. & Heidrich, S.M. (1997), Experience and Well-Being: Explorations on Domains of Life. International Journal of Behavioral Development, 20 (2), 193-206.

Sammartino, F. (1987) The Effect of Health on Retirement. Social Security Bulletin, No. 1.

Segalowitz, S.J. and Davies, P.L. (2004) Charting the Maturation of the Frontal Lobe: An Electrophysiological Strategy. Brain and Cognition, 55, 116-133.

Schaie, K.W. (1985) Longitudinal Studies of Adult Psychological Development. 64-135, Guilford Press, New York.

Schooler, C. (1984) Psychological Effects of Complex Environments During The Life Span: A Review and Theory. Intelligence, 8, 259-281.

Schuler, P., Chodzko-Zajko, W. and Tomporowski, P. (1993) Relationship between Physical Fitness, Age and Attentional Capacity. Research in Sports Medicine, 4 (3), 189-194.
Schwartz, A. (2007) The Health Dangers of Loneliness, Aging and Geriatrics, www.mentalhelp.net/poc/view

Science Daily (2007) Resveratrol Content Varies Among Red Wines. www.sciencedaily.com/releases/2007/04/070419095607.htm

Science Daily (2007) Wine May Combat Tooth Decay and Upper Respiratory Tract Disease. www.sciencedaily.com/releases/2007/06/070625093118.htm

Science Daily (2007) Red Wine Compound Shown to Prevent Prostrate Cancer. www.sciencedaily.com releases/2007/08/070831131320.htm

Science Daily (2007) Red Wine and Grape Juice Help Defend Against Food-Borne Diseases. www.sciencedaily.com/releases/2007/10/071011090436.htm

Science Daily (2008) Grape Skin Compound Fights the Complications of Diabetes. www.sciencedaily.com releases/2008/03/080318094514.htm

Science Daily (2008) Red Wine's Resveratrol May Help Battle Obesity. www.sciencedaily.com/releases/2008/06/080616115850.htm

Science Daily (2008) Substance in Red Wine, Resveratrol, Found to Keep Hearts Young. www.sciencedaily.com/releases/2008/06/080604074908.htm

Science Daily (2008) Cancer Preventative Properties Identified in Resveratrol, Found in Red Wine, Red Grapes. www.sciencedaily.com/releases/2008/07/080707081848.htm

Science Daily (2009) Red Wine Compound Resveratrol Demonstrates Significant Health Benefits.
www.sciencedaily.com/releases/2009/06/090611174052.htm

Science Daily (2009) Scientists Uncork Potential Secret of Red Wine's Health Benefits.
www.sciencedaily.com/releases/2009/07/090730103742.htm

Sears, A. (2008) Seven Steps to a More Youthful Life. http://www.alsearsmd.com

Sears, A. (2008) Telomerase Activation. http://www.telomeraseactivation.org/

Selye, H. (1974) Stress Without Distress, Lippincourt, Philadelphia.

Sitaram, R. et al (2007) FMRI Brain-Computer Interface: A Tool for Neuroscientific Research and Treatment. Computational Intelligence and Neuroscience, Article 1.

Skinner, B.F. (1971) Beyond Freedom and Dignity. Knoph, New York.

Science News (2010) University of Minnesota Research Finds Ovulating Women Unconsciously Buy Sexier Clothing to Outdo Attractive Women. August 04, 2010 Edition.

Somerfeld, L. (2010) Pulling Keys from Elderly Too Painful for Many of Us. Toronto Star, January 30.

Statistics Canada (2007) Canada's Population Future,http: // www41. stat.can.gc.ca/2007/3867/ceb3867001-eng.htm

Statistics Related to Overweight and Obesity. CDC. 2006. http://www.win.niddk.nih.gov/statistics/.

Taylor, P. (2010) Memory Loss Linked to Weight Gain. Globe Life, Globe and Mail, July 16.

Thomas, D. (2003) Selected Poems. New Directions Publishing, New York.

Thompson, P. (1971) What It Means to Be Old Today. Journal of American Geriatric Society, 19 (4), 337-340.

Tierney, M.C., Yao, C, Kiss, A., & McDowell, I. (2005), Neuropsychological Tests Accurately Predict Incident Alzheimer Disease After 5 and 10 Years. Neurology, Vol. 64, 1853-1859.

Vaillant, G.E. (1991) The Association of Ancestral Longevity with Successful Aging. The Journal of Gerontology, Psychological Sciences, 46 (6), 292-298.

Vaillant, G.E. (2002) Aging Well. Little Brown and Company, Boston.

Valliant, P.M. (1980) Injury and Personality Traits in Non-Competitive Runners. The Journal of Sports Medicine and Physical Fitness, 20 (3), 341-346.

Valliant, P.M., & Asu, M.E. (1985) Exercise and Its Effects on Cognition and Physiology in Older Adults, Perceptual and Motor Skills, 61, 1031-1038.

Valliant, P.M. (2009) Nanowired, Trafford, Bloomington, Indiana.

Valliant, P.M. & Furac, C.J. (1993) Type of Housing and Emotional Health of Senior Citizens. Psychological Reports, 73, 1347-1353.

Valliant, P.M., & Leith, B (1986) Impact of Relaxation Training and Cognitive Therapy on Coronary Patients Post Surgery. Psychological Reports, 59, 1271-1278.

Valliant, P.M. & Sombrutski, B. (1974) Lesioning of the Posterior and Medial Hippocampus and its Impact on Later Recall of Task Activity. (Unpublished Study), Lakehead University.

Walford, R. (1983) Maximum Life Span. W.W. Norton, New York.

Warshofsky, F. (1999) Stealing Time. The New Science of Aging, TV Books, New York.

Werner, C., et al. (2009) Beneficial Effects of Long-Term Endurance Exercise on Leukocyte Telomere Biology. Circulation, 120, 492.

Werner, C. et al. (2009) Physical Exercise Prevents Cellular Senescence in Circulating Leukocytes and in the Vessel Wall. Circulation, 120, 2438-2447.

Willauer, E. (2011) The Economics of Retirement. Personal Communication. Department of Economics, Laurentian University.

Wong, P.T. (1989) Personal Meaning and Successful Aging. Canadian Psychology, 30 (3), 516-525.

Yalom, I.D.(1985) The Theory and Practice of Group Psychotherapy. (3rd) Edition, Basic Books, New York.

APPENDIX

NATURAL FOOD, HERBAL SUBSTANCES AND PHARMACEUTICAL DRUGS

I will explore the basis of natural foods, herbal drugs and pharmaceutical supplements which have been found to provide an advantage to health. The natural food products including fruits, vegetables, nuts and grains provide nutritive and non-nutritive chemicals to assist one's health. Many of these natural substances contain phytochemicals which have disease preventative properties. These chemicals are produced by plants as a way of protecting them from diseases. Humans however can also benefit from the disease protective properties. Many phytochemicals have antioxidant ability which offset damage caused by the oxidative process within the cell. It is imperative that people of all ages consume quantities of natural foods with antioxidant ability. These foods are especially of importance to people over the age of 50 whose cells begin to deteriorate during the aging process. Intake of special food groups will ensure longevity.

Phytochemicals:

There are many phytochemicals in naturally occurring food products. Below is a list of some of the more common groups and their benefit to health.

Anthocyanins-

These include the cyanidin and malvidin substances. The cyanidins are present in the skin and juice of berries and fruits. They have beneficial chemical properties which contribute to their anti-carcinogenic, anti-inflammatory ability and reduce the oxidative process allow free radicals to ravage the cells. Malvidin the chemical agent which contributes to the colour of fruit and berries have been implicated in anticancer properties.

Carotenoids-

This group includes the beta-carotenoids, lutein and lycopene substances. Found in coloured fruits and vegetables. These substances are antioxidants and prevent build-up of free radicals which damage the cells. Foods that contain carotenoids serve to protect the cells from cancer and cardiovascular disorders.

Flavonoids-

This group is comprised of a large number of substances including epicatechin, hesperidin, kaempferol, naringin, proanthocyanidins, quercetin, resveratrol, rutin, and tangeretin. These polyphenols have antioxidant properties. They have anti-cancer, anti-viral and anti-inflammatory ability. Quercetin found in many fruits can attack respiratory ailments including asthma, hay fever. The flavonoid group assist in cardiovascular support by preventing low density lipoproteins from building up in blood vessels.

Monoterpenes-
This group includes limone and geraniol. These antioxidants found in the oil byproducts of citrus fruits have anti-cancer properties.

Organosulfides-
This group includes a number of substances with sulphur based properties. The best known of this group includes allicin found in garlic and sulfurophane found in broccoli, cauliflower, cabbage and kale. These substances are antioxidants and can serve to protect the cells from various types of cancer especially those of the prostate and the breast. Other sulphur containing products including avocado, asparagus, grapefruit, spinach and some fruits, strawberry, peach and orange have glutathione which neutralizes free radicals and prevents oxidative damage leading to cell death especially those found in aging individuals as the cells deteriorate.

Phenolic Acid-
These include resveratrol, flavon-3-ols, caffeic acid, ellagic acid, gallic acid, rosmarinic acid and tannic acid. These chemical agents have anti-cancer properties and have been contraindicated in the control of many different forms of cancer especially those of the colon, liver, skin and lungs. Other phenolic compounds including catechins, flavonols, tannins and anthocyanins prevent oxidative damage. Some phenolics including salicylic and hydrobenzoic apparently attack viruses and bacteria.

NATURAL FOODS

FRUITS:
The nutrient and non-nutrients obtained from the below listed foods are based on the USDA nutrient values charts. These have been charted in food products with a quantity of 100 grams. Nutrients, vitamins or minerals above 1 mcg per 100 were included but the list may not be exhaustive of all possible substances. Fruits contain antioxidant substances including carotenoids, these can assist in warding off cancer. Many fruits also contain flavonoids (proanthocyanidins) which are useful in reducing risk of coronary heart disease by suppressing the protein edothelin-1 which constricts blood vessels. Proanthocyanidins also have antioxidant activity which stabilize collagen and elastin, two proteins found in organs, blood vessels, joints, connective tissue and muscle.

Acerola Cherry-
Powerful antioxidant containing high levels of vitamin C; approximately 32 times more than an equal portion of orange juice.

Apple-
A raw medium apple with skin is a good source of calcium, magnesium, phosphorus, potassium, choline, vitamin C, folate, vitamin A, beta-carotene, lutein, vitamin K. An apple contains an antioxidant known as flavonoids. This substance is useful in reducing the chance of developing diabetes and asthma.

Apricot-
A raw apricot is a good source of calcium, magnesium, phosphorus, potassium, vitamin A, folate, choline, beta- carotene, alpha-carotene, lutein, vitamin E, vitamin K.

Avocado-
A good source of calcium, magnesium, phosphorus, potassium, vitamin A, selenium, niacin, folate, choline, vitamin A, beta carotene, alpha carotene, crytoxanthin, vitamin E, and vitamin K.

Banana-
A medium raw banana is a good source of calcium, magnesium, phosphorus. potassium, selenium, vitamin C, folate, choline, vitamin A, beta-carotene, alpha carotene, vitamin A, lutein.

Berries-
Contain proanthocyanidins, antioxidants which prevent cancer and heart disease.

Bilberry-
European berry with high levels of phytochemicals, anthocyanins and polyphenols; stabilize the walls of blood vessels especially the capillaries; maintain the integrity of the blood vessels of the retina for improved eyesight and preserve the eye against macular degeneration, retinopathy, retinitis pigmentosa and reduces poor night vision.

Blackberries-
One hundred grams of raw berries contain calcium, magnesium, phosphorus, potassium, vitamin C, folate, choline, vitamin A, beta-carotene, lutein, vitamin E, tocopherol, vitamin K. Contain anthocyanin which is useful in preventing cancer, and cardiovascular disease, especially heart disease and stroke. Flavonoids strengthen the blood vessels. The leaves can be made into a tea to treat sore throats and mouth cankers.

Blueberries-
One hundred grams of blueberries are a good source of calcium, magnesium, phosphorus, potassium, manganese, vitamin C, vitamin A, beta-carotene, alpha-carotene, vitamin A. The blueberry plant is a good source of antioxidants with the phytochemicals anthocyanidins, flavonoids, resveratrol, anthocyanins, and ellagic acid. These antioxidants inhibit free radicals and assist in preventing diseases including, heart disease, cancer, varicose veins. haemorrhoids, peptic ulcers. These berries also prevent bacteria from adhering to the lining of the bladder preventing urinary tract infections. The Natives in North America dried the leaves and used them to make tea to treat sore throat, mouth and oral infections.

Cranberry-
One hundred grams of cranberry juice is a good source of antioxidants especially catechins, hippuric acid and anthocyanins. The antioxidant hippuric acid has anti-adhesion properties which reduce the ability of bacteria adhering to membranes, thus limiting bacteria and infections to the urinary tract and ulcers in the stomach. A good source of calcium, magnesium, phosphorous, potassium, vitamin C, folate, choline, vitamin A,

beta-carotene, lutein, vitamin E, vitamin K.

Currants-

One hundred grams of dried currants are a good source of calcium, iron, magnesium, phosphorus, potassium, vitamin C, niacin, folate, choline, vitamin A, beta- carotene, vitamin K. Phytochemicals in these fruits include anthocyanidins flavonoids, quercetin, and kaempferol. The anthocyanidins serve to protect by their antioxidant and antibacterial ability. The Hopi natives made a tea from the leaves to increase urinary flow and dissipate fever.

Raisins-

One hundred grams of dried seedless raisins are a good source of calcium, iron, magnesium, phosphorus, potassium, vitamin C, folate, choline, vitamin K.

Raspberries-

One hundred grams of raw raspberries are a good source of calcium, magnesium, phosphorus, potassium, vitamin C, folate, choline, vitamin A, beta-carotene, alpha-carotene, lutein, tocopherol and vitamin K. Have elevated levels of ellagic acid an antioxidant which may assist in reducing various types of cancer (ie. cervical, oesophageal and colon).

Strawberries-

One hundred grams of raw strawberries are a good source of calcium, magnesium, phosphorus, potassium, folate, choline, vitamin K. Wild strawberries have an abundance of cyanidin and ellagic acid. Strawberry consumption can reduce the risk of cancer cells specifically in colon and breast. The leaves of this plant have tannins and ellagitannins, proanthyocyanins, flavonoids, salicylic acid, caffeic acids. Tea made with the leaves can be used to treat dysentery and diarrhoea.

Cantaloupe-
One hundred grams of raw cantaloupe is a good source calcium, magnesium, phosphorus, potassium, vitamin C, folate, beta-carotene, alpha carotene, vitamin A, lutein, vitamin K.

Grapefruit-
One medium red or pink grapefruit is a good source of calcium, magnesium, phosphorous, potassium, selenium, folate, vitamin A. Contains a flavonoid known as nargenin; antioxidant acts by binding to toxins and removing them from the body. Pink grapefruit contains lycopene a carotenoid which counteracts free radical damage.

Grapes-
Green or Red-
One hundred grams of raw grapes is a good source of calcium, magnesium, phosphorous, vitamin K, vitamin C, folate, choline, vitamin A, beta-carotene, alpha-carotene, vitamin K. Grapes have a number of phytochemicals including flavonoids, resveratrol, quercetin, anthocyanins, kaempferol, cyanidin, ellagic acid and proanthocyanidins. Flavonoids assist in reducing risk of cancer. In combination the flavonoids, ellagic acid and resveratrol prevent heart disease. Quercetin assists in reducing impact of free radicals by inhibiting the oxidative process. Proanthocyanidins found in the grape seeds assist diabetics with their vascular systems.

Muscadine-
One hundred grams of raw grapes is a good source of calcium, magnesium, phosphorus, potassium, folate, vitamin A, beta-carotene, alpha-carotene, lutein. These grapes apparently produce higher levels or resveratrol during the fermentation process.

Mango-
One medium raw fruit is a good source of calcium, manganese, phosphorus, potassium, vitamin C, folate, choline, beta-carotene, alpha-carotene, vitamin A, lycopene, lutein, vitamin K.

Olive-
Olives contain antioxidant phytochemicals hydroxytyrosol and oleuropein. These substances prevent hyperglycemia and oxidative stress of diabetes. Oleuropein apparently has anti-tumour ability and reduce the risk of cancer.

Orange-
One medium raw florida orange is a good source of calcium, magnesium, phosphorus, potassium, vitamin C, folate, choline, vitamin A, beta-carotene, alpha-carotene, crypto-xanthin, vitamin A, lutein. This fruit has a number of phytochemicals including carotenoids, isohesperidin, terpineol, narigin, limonin, flavonoids, hesperidin, and limonene. Flavonoids and limonene have anticancer properties which inhibit tumour growth. Limonin and limonene have detoxifying properties. Peel of the skin is replete with vitamin C which can be dried and grated to make tea.

Papaya-
One small fruit contains calcium, magnesium, phosphorus, potassium, vitamin C, thiamin, riboflavin, niacin, pantothenic acid, vitamin B6, folate, beta-carotene, alpha-carotene, cryptoxanthin, lycopene, vitamin A, lutein, tocopherol, vitamin k. Contains papain which aid in digestion.

Peach-
One large raw peach contains calcium, magnesium, phosphorous, potassium, vitamin C, folate, choline, vitamin A, beta-carotene, crytoxanthin, lutein, vitamin K.

Pear-
One medium raw pear contains calcium, magnesium, phosphorous, potassium, vitamin C, folate, choline, vitamin A, beta-carotene, lutein and vitamin K.

Pineapple-
One hundred grams of raw traditional pineapple contains calcium, magnesium, phosphorus, potassium, manganese, vitamin C, folate, choline, vitamin A, beta-carotene. Contains bromelain which prevents cancer, blood clots, aids in digestion.

Pomegranate-
One medium size pomegranate contains calcium, magnesium, phosphorous, potassium, vitamin C, folate, choline, Vitamin K. Pomegranate juice contains anthocyanis, cyanidin and ellagic acid. The juice is a mild astringent, can be used to treat diarrhoea, root bark is used to treat intestinal parasites especially tapeworm. Ellagic acid is used to fight various cancers and fibrosis activity.

Prunes (Dried Plums)-
One hundred grams of dried fruit contains calcium, magnesium, phosphorous, potassium, folate, choline, vitamin A, beta-carotene, alpha-carotene, crypotoxanthin, vitamin A, lutein, vitamin K.

GRAINS, NUTS AND SEEDS:

Almond-
This fruit contains a number of phytochemicals including methylquercetin, catechin, vanillic acid, flavonoids, resveratrol, kaempferol. High calcium levels reduce risk of colon and rectal cancer; high levels of flavonoids in the skin inhibit oxidation of low density lipoproteins (LDL), reducing formation of plaques in the arteries and lowers cholesterol levels.

Flaxseed-
Seven grams (one tablespoon) of ground flaxseed contains calcium, iron, magnesium, phosphorous, potassium, zinc, copper, manganese, selenium, thiamin, niacin, folate, choline, betaine, lutein, tocopherol, vitamin K. This seed provides a rich supply of alpha-linolenic acid and lignans. It assists as an anti-cancer agent and assists in lowering blood cholesterol because of its high content of omega-3 fatty acids. Is also used to offset irritable colon problems and to reduce constipation.

Oats-
One hundred grams of oats contains calcium, iron, magnesium, phosphorous, potassium, zinc, manganese, pantothenic acid, folate.

Sesame Seeds-
Nine grams (one tablespoon) of dried seeds contains calcium, iron, magnesium, phosphorous, potassium, zinc, copper, manganese, selenium, niacin, folate, choline, beta-carotene, vitamin A.

Walnuts-
One hundred grams of walnuts contains calcium, iron, magnesium, phosphorous, potassium, zinc, copper, manganese, selenium, vitamin C, niacin, folate, choline, vitamin A, beta-carotene, lutein, tocopherol, vitamin K.

VEGETABLES

Arame-
This plant contains vitamin A, calcium, iodine, iron, magnesium.

Artichokes- A raw medium artichoke contains calcium, iron, magnesium, phosphorus, vitamin C, niacin, folate choline, potassium, bet-carotene, vitamin A, lutein, vitamin K.

Asparagus-
Good source of vitamin B6, calcium, magnesium, zinc, vitamin A, C, E, K, thiamin, riboflavin, niacin, iron phosphorus, potas-

sium, copper, manganese, selenium; contains folate which is instrumental in removing homocysteine from cells; prevents neural defect in fetus, and heart related disorders.

Beet-
One hundred grams of this boiled vegetable has a variety of healthful substances including calcium, iron, magnesium, phosphorus, potassium, zinc, copper, manganese, vitamin C, thiamin, riboflavin, niacin, folate, vitamin A, beta-carotene.

Broccoli-
This vegetable contains a number of phytochemicals including glucosinolates, dithiolthiones, indoles, glucoraphanin, s-methyl cyteine sulfoxide, isothicyanates, and indole-3-carbinol. This vegetable is thought to have cardiovascular protective properties, anti-cancer and anti-helicobacteria ability, the bacteria which are thought to lead to stomach ulcers.

Cabbage-
One hundred grams of common boiled cabbage has calcium, iron, magnesium, potassium, phosphorus, zinc, manganese, vitamin, C, thiamin, riboflavin, niacin, vitamin B, folate, choline, beta-carotene, vitamin K.

Carrots-
One hundred grams of raw carrot contains calcium, iron, magnesium, phosphorus, potassium, zinc, copper, manganese, vitamin C. thiamin, riboflavin, niacin, vitamin B6, choline, betaine, Vitamin A, vitamin K. Carrots contain beta-carotenoids, antioxidants which remove free radicals; these assist in warding off cancer and cardiovascular disease.

Cauliflower-
This vegetable is a good source of calcium, magnesium, phosphorous, potassium, zinc, copper, manganese, vitamin c, thiamin, riboflavin, niacin, folate, vitamin B6, vitamin A.

Garlic-
The bulbs of garlic contain flavonoids and sulphur like compounds (diallyl sulphate, ajoene and allicin). The active ingredient allicin attacks viruses and bacteria; good to treat allergies, asthma, bronchitis, cold sores; prevents the blood from thickening, prevents high blood pressure; contains anti-inflammatory properties to relieve pain; lowers cholesterol and blood lipid levels; allicin and ajoene prevent aggregation of platelets thereby reducing risk of stroke.

Kale-
One hundred grams of boiled kale is a good source of calcium, iron, magnesium, phosphorous, potassium, copper, zinc, manganese, selenium, vitamin C, thiamin, riboflavin, niacin, folate, choline, betain, vitamin A, lutein, vitamin E, carotene

Leeks-
One hundred grams of raw leek contain calcium, iron, magnesium, phosphorous, potassium, zinc, copper, manganese, selenium, vitamin C, thiamin, riboflavin, niacin, vitamin B6, folate, vitamin A, beta-carotene, lutein, and vitamin E.

Peppers-
Green, Red, Yellow – Contain calcium ,iron, magnesium, phosphorous, potassium, zinc, copper, manganese, vitamin C, thiamin, riboflavin, niacin, pantothenic acid, folate, choline,

beta-carotene, alpha carotene, vitamin A, vitamin E, vitamin K.

Sweet Potatoes-
Contain beta-carotenoids, and antioxidants which remove free radicals; assist in warding of cancer and cardiovascular disease.

Radishes-
One hundred grams of raw radish contain calcium, iron, magnesium, phosphorus, copper, manganese, vitamin C, thiamin, riboflavin, niacin, folate, choline, B12, vitamin A, lutein, vitamin K.

Spinach-
One hundred grams of raw spinach is a good source of calcium, iron, magnesium, phosphorous, potassium, zinc, copper, manganese, selenium, vitamin C, thiamin, riboflavin, niacin, pantothenic acid, folate, choline, betaine, vitamin A, beta carotene, vitamin A, vitamin E, vitamin K.

Tomato-
One medium whole tomato contains calcium, magnesium, phosphorous, potassium, vitamin C, folate, choline, vitamin A, beta-carotene, vitamin A, lutein, vitamin K. Contains a number of phytochemicals including flavonoids, carotenoids, lycopene, quercetin, polyphenols, kaempferol. Lycopene a carotenoid is the most healthful of the antioxidants. It removes free radicals and assists in warding off cancers including prostrate cancer by increasing the production of the luciferase enzyme.

Wakame-
Good source of omega-3; also contains calcium, thiamin, niacin, iodine.

FISH:
There are many species of fish. These include Cod, Haddock, Halibut, Perch, Pike, Sardines, Salmon, Trout and Walleye. These species are a good source of protein, vitamins and minerals. Certain species including the salmon, and trout family, live in deep water; they are a good source of Omega 3 fatty acid, Eicosapentaenoic (EPA) acid and Docosahexaenoic (DPA) acid. Fish also have an abundance of other healthy nutrients including calcium, iron, magnesium, phosphorus, potassium, zinc, copper, manganese, selenium, vitamin C, thiamin, riboflavin, niacin, pantothenic acid, vitamin B6, folate, choline, vitamin B12, vitamin A, retinol, vitamin E, vitamin D; Amino acids are the main components of protein. The specific amino acids in fish include: tryptophan, threonine, isoleucine, leucine, lysine, methionine, cystine, phenylalanine, tyrosine, valine, arginine, histidine, aspartic acid, glutamic acid, glycine, proline and serine.

MEAT:
There has been much controversy regarding meat products. Many argue that organic (free range) animals are allowed to graze freely and therefore are not fed a host of substances including growth hormones, antibiotics or animal chows which affect the quality of the meat. One must keep in mind that animals raised in the wilds probably are the only true "free range - organic products" available for consumption. Inspection of the USDA - Agricultural National Nutrient

Database indicates that free range meat is high in a number of nutrient elements.

Free Range/Wild Animals.

Bear- 100 grams of cooked meat has 32.4 grams of protein and 10.7 grams of iron. Other nutrients include magnesium, phosphorous, potassium, zinc, copper, selenium, thiamin, riboflavin, niacin, vitamin B6, folate, choline, betain, vitamin B12, vitamin E, vitamin K.

Deer- 100 grams of cooked meat has 30.2 grams of protein and 4.7 grams of iron. Other nutrients include magnesium, phosphorous, potassium, zinc, copper, manganese, selenium, thiamin, riboflavin, niacin.

Elk- 100 grams of cooked meat has 30.2 grams of protein and 3.6 grams of iron. Other nutrients include calcium, magnesium, phosphorous, potassium, zinc, copper, manganese, selenium, folate.

Moose- 100 grams of cooked meat has 29.3 grams of protein and 4.2 grams of iron. Other nutrients include calcium, magnesium, phosphorous, potassium, zinc, copper, manganese, selenium, vitamin C, thiamin, riboflavin, niacin, vitamin B6, folate, choline, betaine, vitamin B12, vitamin E, vitamin K.

Rabbit- 100 grams of cooked meat has 30 grams of protein and 4.9 grams of iron. Other nutrients include calcium, magnesium, phosphorous, potassium, zinc, copper, selenium, thiamin, riboflavin, niacin, vitamin B6, folate, choline, betaine, B12, vitamin E, vitamin K.

Domesticated Animals.

Beef- 100 grams of roast beef has 25.7 grams of protein and 1.7 grams of iron. Other nutrients include calcium, magnesium, phosphorous, potassium, zinc, copper, manganese, selenium, thiamin, riboflavin, niacin, pantothenic acid, vitamin B6.

Chicken- 100 grams of roast chicken has 26 grams of protein and 1.4 grams of iron. Other nutrients include calcium, magnesium, phosphorous, potassium, zinc, copper, manganese, selenium, thiamin, riboflavin, niacin, pantothenic acid, vitamin B6, folate, choline, betain, vitamin B12, vitamin A, vitamin, E, vitamin D, vitamin K.

Lamb- 100 grams of cooked meat has 33.7 grams of protein and 2.8 grams of iron. Other nutrients include calcium, magnesium, phosphorous, potassium, zinc, copper, manganese, selenium, thiamin, riboflavin, niacin, pantothenic acid, vitamin B6, folate, choline, betaine, vitamin B12, vitamin, D, vitamin E, vitamin K.

Pork- 100 grams of roasted meat has 20.4 grams of protein and and 0.95 grams of iron. Other nutrients include calcium, magnesium, phosphorous, potassium, zinc, copper, manganese, selenium, thiamin, riboflavin, niacin, pantothenic acid, vitamin B6, folate, choline, betaine, vitamin E. vitamin D.

Rabbit- 100 grams of cooked meat has 30 grams of protein and 2.4 grams of iron. Other nutrients include calcium, magnesium, phosphorous, potassium, zinc, copper, manganese, selenium, thiamin, riboflavin, niacin, pantothenic acid, vitamin B6, folate, choline, betain, vitamin E, vitamin K.

HERBAL SUBSTANCES

HERBS:
Herbal medicines have been around for centuries. Below are a list of some of the types used in cooking and for medicinal purposes. Many people use some of these in culinary preparation. These should only be used prior to consultation with a qualified medical doctor to ensure that one is using it wisely.

Astragalus-
Chinese herb known to strengthen the immune system and the heart; increases telomerase to reduce telomere deterioration; creates white blood cells and interferon to ward of cancer.

Capsicum-
Circulatory stimulant and analgesic; found in chili peppers.

Cayenne-
Part of the chili pepper family; high in vitamins A, B6, E, C, riboflavin, potassium and manganese; good as an antiseptic for treating wounds and stimulating blood circulation.

Celery Seed-
Lowers the blood concentration of uric acid; has anti-inflammatory properties; reduce hypertension because it contains apigenin; reduces arthritis, inflammation and regulates the heart to prevent arrhythmia.

Cacao Bean (Chocolate)-
Has a number of phytochemicals including flavonols, flavonoids, quercetin, caffeine, theobromine. This substance has a number of uses; provides an energy boost by stimulating the CNS. The xanthines in the bean have a vasodilation effect thus increasing flow of blood.

Echinacea-
Active ingredients caffeic acid, cichoric acid and echinacoside provide the antibacterial, antiviral and immune enhancing properties; used to treat colds and the flu.

Epimedium (Horny Goat Weed/Yin Yang Huo)-
Flowering plant endemic to China. This plant is alleged to have aphrodisiac qualities. Increases levels of nitric oxide and relaxes smooth muscle. The active ingredient icarin acts similarly to the drug sildenafil (Viagra) to enhance erections.

Evening Primrose-
Contain quercetin; assists in the treatment of asthma; used to treat prostrate problems and urinary difficulties; Assists recovering alcoholics by reducing withdrawal effects; used by women to treat premenstrual difficulties.

Fucoxanthin-
Seaweed extract which activates a protein UCP1 to burn fat cells.

Ginger-
This plant has pain killing properties, antibacterial and sedative properties; has been found to kill ovarian cancer cells; decreases arthritic pain, blood thinning and reduces cholesterol; used to treat heart disease. .

Ginseng (Korean)-
Believed to enhance the immune system and increase energy; noted to assist in preventing cancer.

Green Tea-
Contains high levels of flavonoids a group of phytochemicals known to have anti-oxidative effects; lowers incidence of heart; increase burning of body fats; contains vitamin C, chromium, manganese, selenium, zinc; can reduce the risk of cardiovascular disease, kidney stones, cancer and improves bone density; reduces systolic and diastolic blood pressure.

Hawthorn-
Powerful heart medication; used to treat cardiovascular problems including angina, has beta-blocking properties to lower blood pressure and increase blood flow, can stabilize heart rhythm.

Irvingia Gabonensis-
African herb assists in burning body fat.

Maca-

This biennial plant is found in the Andes mountains of Peru. It serves as a medicinal herb. It contains sugars, proteins, uridine, malic acid, glucosinolates, glucotropelin and methoxyglucotropaeol. It is also rich in selenium, calcium, magnesium, iron, , linolenic acid, palmitic acid, oleic acid, and 19 amino acids. Used to provide added energy and enhanced libido. In males it can improve sperm production, sperm motility and semen volume.

Maitake Mushrooms-

Has a number of vitamins, B2, D2, niacin and , minerals including potassium, calcium, magnesium and beta glucan which enhances the immune system; also contains many antioxidants.

Milk Thistle-

The phytochemicals in this plant include flavonoids and silymarin. The active ingredient silymarin prevents toxins from entering the liver cells and removes the toxins which build up in the liver; this is a useful medicinal agent that can assist those who drink too much alcohol and need to detoxify.

Paullinia cupana-

The active compound in this seed is guaranine, a product of the caffeine family. This substance contains fatty acids leading to slow release of the chemical. This substance energizes and revitalizes the body without the side effects of coffee including nervousness or anxiety. This substance releases acetylcholine into the brain causing enhanced memory and mental sharpness.

Reishi Mushrooms-
Enhance the immune system, used to fight tumours, and lower blood pressure and cholesterol.

Rosemary-
High in vitamin B6, calcium and iron; has been thought to lower free radicals in the body and brain. Contains phytochemicals rosmarinic acid, flavonoids and limonene. Can be used to increase blood circulation, treat headaches, colds.

Sage-
Contains the phytochemicals flavonoids, rosmarinic acid and tannins. This herb has a number of medicinal properties which include anti-septic, stimulant, anti-spasmodic. It was used by Natives to dissipate upset stomach, reduce mouth ulcers, cankers, sore gums and swollen tonsils. Used in the treatment of gallbladder and liver problems.

Shitake Mushrooms-
This mushroom increases resistance to viruses and bacteria by increasing levels of interferon and increasing T cells, lymphocytes necessary for combating cancer.

St. John's Wort-
This herb contains hypericin, pseudohypericin, protohypericin and hyperforin. One active agent hypericin is an anti-inflammatory and antibiotic useful when applied to skin related disorders. This substance has also been used to treat mood related disorder, irritability, fatigue, and disturbances in sleeping and eating.

Saw Palmetto-
Assists in reducing benign prostrate enlargement; improves urinary flow.

Thyme-
Contains thymol used as an antiseptic; used for respiratory infections or inflammation of the throat.

Tumeric-
Contains many antioxidants including vitamin C and E to remove free radicals; used also as an anti-inflammatory; prevents colon, lung and breast cancer.

Valerian-
Is a flowering plant believed to have sedative and anxiolytic (reduction of anxiety) effects.

NATURAL SOURCES OF VITAMINS AND MINERALS OR SYNTHETIC PHARMACEUTICALS

Vitamins and Minerals can be obtained from organic material; vitamins are produced by the plant and minerals acquired by absorption of minerals from the soils in which the plant grows. Synthetic production of vitamins and minerals has become a multi-billion dollar industry driven by consumers. The best source of vitamins and minerals is through the consumption of food products in their natural state. The quick pace of life has prevented the masses from taking time to consume natural products. In their haste synthetic sources are used. According to research scientists the best source of vitamins and minerals are products in their natural state. These are better assimilated by the body.

MINERALS:
These nutrients are noted to be inorganic in nature and are acquired by plants from the soil in which they grow. Consumption of plant material will provide one with a supply of minerals.

Boron-
This trace mineral is necessary for the metabolism of calcium, magnesium and hormones. This nutrient is important in the formation of bone, muscle mass and proper functioning of the prostrate gland. Deficiency in this nutrient is implicated in arthritis and testosterone levels in the elderly. Can be obtained in fruits, nuts, leafy vegetables and red wine.

Calcium-
This mineral is necessary for bone formation, utilization of iron and for nutrient passage into cells.

Copper-
Copper allows for iron absorption and mobilization. This mineral plays a role in the formation of collagen, elastin and connective tissue. Insufficient copper leads to weak bones and defects in blood vessel walls.

Folate-
This mineral assists in the production of red blood cells, cell growth, prevention of neural tube defects (eg. spina bifida), reduction of homocysteine in the cells.

Iodine-
This mineral assists in proper functioning of the thyroid gland by increasing levels of thyroxin; assists in the metabolism of fatty substances, and in the formation of bones, skin nails, hair and teeth.

Iron-
This mineral is necessary to form haemoglobin in the blood. Haemoglobin transports oxygen to the cells in the body. This substance is necessary for cell growth.

Magnesium-
This mineral is necessary for proper blood circulation, building and strengthening of bones, heart and muscle regulation.

Manganese-
This mineral is important for a number of specific body functions including assisting other nutrients (biotin, thiamin, ascorbic acid and choline) in doing their jobs; it also is used to strengthen bones, main normal blood sugar levels, synthesize fatty acids and assist in proper functioning of the nervous system.

Phosphorous-
This mineral is essential for cell growth and repair; it assists the body in utilization of proteins, carbohydrates and fats. It assists in the neurotransmission of impulses.

Potassium-

This mineral is used by the cells in the process of neurotransmission. It assist with coordination of nerve impulses and proper electrolyte balance; assists with muscle contraction and in the reduction of blood pressure.

Selenium-

This mineral binds to proteins to make selenoproteins to form antioxidant properties in the cell. Selenium removes free radicals, substances which cause cell damage. Assist in the regulation of the thyroid gland, and immune system.

Zinc-

This mineral is important for metabolism within the cell and plays a role in protein and DNA/RNA synthesis, cell division, andsupports immune functioning.

VITAMINS:

These nutrients are produced in plants. Consumption of plants provides the consumer with daily requirements.

A (Retinol)-

This vitamin is required for maintenance of organ systems especially the skin, glands, mucous membranes, hair. The production of rhodopsin and iodopsin allows for night and colour vision. This substance elevates the immune system to ward of infections and diseases, assists in growth and metabolism.

Betaine-
This nutrient is a methyl donor which infers that it assists chemical processes in the body. Assists the liver to do its job of processing other nutrients. Lowers levels of homocysteine.

B1 (Thiamin)-
This vitamin is necessary for the integrity of the nervous system, heart and muscles.

B2 (Riboflavin)-
This vitamin is necessary for growth of red blood cells, functioning of the nervous system, assists in breakdown of food and the utilization of the other B vitamins especially B3, B6 and vitamin K.

B3 (Niacin)-
This vitamin is necessary for the integrity and function of the nervous system, metabolism of protein, carbohydrate and fat and conversion of food to energy.

B6 (Pyridoxine)-
This vitamin is necessary for proper immune and nervous system function. It is involved in metabolism of protein and the underlying amino acids. It assists in building the red blood cells and allows the hormones to be synthesized by the body.

B7 (Biotin)-
Assists in energy production by converting glucose and lipids (fatty acids). Assists in metabolizing other food intake especially proteins, carbohydrates and fats.

B9 (Folic Acid)-
This vitamin is important for the proper formation of the brain and spinal cord. Assists with the formation of the DNA nucleic acids, intestinal tract and in the metabolism of amino acids.

B12 (Cobalamin)-
This vitamin assists in forming the red blood cell. It assists in forming the nucleic acid in the DNA complex. Allows the cells in the CNS, PNS, and ANS nervous system to function. Prevents homocysteine build-up in the cell thereby acting as an anti-aging substance.

C (L-ascorbic acid)-
This vitamin is one of the most important for the integral functioning of the organ, nervous and immune systems. Essential for healthy gums which support the teeth. Assists in the formation of supportive structures including skin, bones, and formation of blood vessels.

Choline-
This vitamin is synthesized to produce acetylcholine a neurotransmitter which assists in muscle control and enhancement of memory.

D-
Vitamin D is necessary for improved cognition. Low levels have been linked to problems with memory, thinking and learning. Administration of this substance has also been approved as a means of reducing dementia.

E (Tocopherol)-
This vitamin is important for bone formation; it assist in the metabolism and absorption of calcium and phosphorous by the body.

K (Phylloquinone/Menaquinone)-
This vitamin allows for the synthesis of proteins/amino acids; serves as a blood clotting factor.

Pantothenic Acid-
This vitamin is necessary for the regulation of neurotransmitters and release of hormones. It assists the body in converting proteins, carbohydrates and fats into energy.

OTHER SUPPLEMENTS:

Bee Pollen-
This substance contains over a 100 different nutrients (eg. amino acids, vitamins, minerals, trace elements, enzymes and coenzymes) and 35 grams of protein. It contains all the elements to sustain life.

Chondroitin-
This substance benefits the body by allowing water into the cells which carries nutrients. It makes connective tissue more shock absorbent and protects cartilage from deterioration.

Coenzyme Q10-
This fat soluble agent is a powerful antioxidant and in combination with Vitamin E increases the body's energy source by

powering up the ATP cycle. It prevents oxidization of low density lipoproteins (LDL) which lead to atherosclerosis. It strengthens the heart, reduces hypertension and boosts the immune system.

Glucosamine-
This substance produces gylcosaminoglycan a molecule used in the formation and repair of cartilage.

L-Arginine-
This is one of the essential amino acids in the body. This substance is a precursor to nitric oxide a substance which increases blood circulation and sexual function. This substance has also been found to improve immune function, stimulate growth hormone, reduce blood clots and/or stroke and to improve vascular function in those with angina.

INDEX

A

Abkhazia	25
Abrahamsen, D.	60
Acceptance	62
ACTH	90
Adrenalin	90
Aging	
positive	4, 12, 22
process	30, 37, 42
Alekoumbides	43
Allicin	80
Alzheimer Disease	80
Alpha Lipoic Acid	82
Ancestral Longevity	58
Androgen	104
Andropause	104
Amygdala	51
Antioxidants	70
Apoe e 4 allele	50
Arteriosclerosis	40
Astragalus	29, 81
Attitude	
Optimistic	4
Aubert, G.	28

B

Bandura, A.	61
Bacteria	35
Baker, L.	41
Baseline Data	31
Beach, F.	106
Beer	85
Bell, A.G.	148

Bisphenol A 85
Blazer, D. 158
Blood Pressure 25
Botwinick, J. 39
Bortz, W. 105
Brain
    dominant 20
    frontal 30, 40
    left 20
    lobes 42
    right 20

C

Canada Food Guide 83
CanDrive Project 15
Carbohydrates 40
Cardiovascular 40
Cattell, R. 39
Cell Deterioration 37
Centenarians 25, 31
Cerebral Cortex 20, 30, 39
Charter, R. 43
Chilton, D. 120
Chodzko-Zajko, W. 78
Chromosomes 27
Cialis 106
Clarke, J. 56
Coenzyme Q10 80
Cognition 31
Cognitive
    activities 2, 30
    behavioral 30, 32
    decline 31
    decrements 31, 40
    deterioration 2
    processing 30, 37

INDEX

strategies	43
therapy	93
training	66
Coles, T.	157
Comprehension	42
Confabulation	38
Conversation	
tracking	38
two person	38
Cooperberg, C.	118
Cortex	30
Cortical Activity	66
Cortisol	37, 90
Covey, R.	65
Craik, F.	44
Cravit, D.	66
Croisile, B.	66

D

Davies, P.	30
Dawkins, R.	154
Decision Making	31
Dekosky, S.	81
Dementia	30
Dendrites	30
Devries, W.	164
Diagnostic Care	31
Dixon, R.	44
DNA	18, 50
DNA Complex	51
Dobbs, A.	16
Downey, A.	151
DriveAble	16
Duke, J.	70
Dunn, M.	110, 111
Durante, K.	110

Dysfunctional   67, 68

E
Echinacea   80
Emotional
    stability   60
    support   61
Empty Nest   89
Endorphins   76
Ephedrine   107
Erber, J.   44
Erikson, E.   10, 61-67, 89, 94
Estrogen   51, 102
Exercise
    daily   71, 72, 76
    programs   28, 59, 73, 74, 78
    trainer   75

F
Fast Foods   36
Feifel, H.   152
Fisher, B.   57
Folic Acid   82
Foner, A.   150
Formative Period   60
Frankl, V.   155
Free Radicals   29, 70, 82
Freud, S.   99
Frikke-Schmidt, R.   50
Fruits   190-197

G
Gebhard, P.   99

Genes	19
bad	26
good	26
Genealogy	31
Genetic	
markers	26
variability	26
Genome Project	148
Ginkgo Biloba	81
Gilman, A.	82
Glasser, A.	93
Gold, C.	55
Gold, D.	68
Golden Age	17
Goodman, L.	82
Grains, Nuts, Seeds	197-198
Gray, G.	57
Gray, P.	109

H

Hawkley, L.	52, 142
Hayflick, L.	28
Health	
emotional	10.20
physical	10, 20
Heiman, J.	107
Herbal Substances	205-210
Higginbottom, S.	5, 115
Hippocampus	38, 51, 52
Hirschman, J.	164
Holden, K.	114
Homocysteine	81
Hormone Replacement	52
Houx, P.	42
Hunza	25
Hypothalamus	90

I

Imitation	61
Immune System	5, 35, 80
Imprinting	61
Intelligence	
ability	30
crystallized	31
fluid	39
quotient	31

J

Johnson, V.	100
Jolles, J.	42
Jung, C.	110

K

Keith, P.	118
Kinsberg, S.	100, 101
Kinsey, A.	99
Koren, G.	X111
Koren, S.	1X
Krause, N.	115
Kubler-Ross, E.	95

L

Lansdorp, P.	28
Launois, J.	25, 26, 70
Laurin, D.	77
Leaf, A.	25, 26, 70
Leith, B.	93
Leming, M.	152
Levy, J.	105

INDEX

Lewin, K.	69
Life Expectancy	35
Lineage	26
Locus of Control	119
Logue, B.	122
Lorenz, K.	61
Lutein	82
Lycopene	82

M

Marconi, G.	148
Markides, K.	158
Marshall, S.	15
Maslow, A.	22, 63
Masters, W.	100
Martin, C.	99
McConnell, J.	50, 51
Meat	202-205
Memory	18, 30, 31
delayed	46
distant	44
potential	52
recall	38
recent	44, 46
working	44
Menopause	51, 102, 103
Meston, C.	101, 107
Methuselah Enzyme	27
Minerals	210-213
Mitochondria	4, 35
Modelling	61
Mor-Barat, M.	116
Morley, J.	103
Murphy, D.	37
Myerson, J.	38

N

Nagy, V.	152
Natural Foods	190-210
Neugarten, B.	79, 116
Neural	
network	30
pathways	41
Neuroimaging	41
Neurons	
connections	30
cortical	30
growth	30
Neuropsychological	50
Nkongolo, K.	28
Nussbaum, M.	103

O

Optimists	7
Organ Systems	31, 35, 42
Overweight	36
Oxidation	35
Oxytocin	110

P

Palmore, E.	57, 158
Park, D.	40, 41
Pate, R.	72
Pathogens	35
Peale, N.V.	152, 154
Perls, T.	26
Persinger, M.	154
Personality	74
Pessimists	7
Peters, R.	142

Pharmaceutical	51
Physical	
ability	3
activity	3
Physician	31
Phytochemical	80, 188-189
Pituitary	37
Planaria	50
Plasticity	30
Polysaturated Fats	40
Pomeroy, W.	99
Positive	
self-worth	60
thoughts	7
Processing	
reaction time	30
speed	31
Prognostic Care	31
Prosocial Behavior	61
Psychodynamic	60
Psychological	30
Pulliam Weston, L.	113

Q
Quirouette, C.	68

R
Rappaport, M.	15
Reasoning	31
Reckler, G.	56
Relaxation	93
Reminiscing	17
Restorative	36
Resveratrol	86

Riboflavin	82
Riley, M.	158
Roosendaal, B.	51
Roos, L.	56
Roos, N.	56
Rotter, J.	119
RRSP	119
Ryff, C.	57

S

Sammartino, F.	118
Saturated Fats	36
Schaie, W.	41, 43
Schwartz, A.	142
Sears, A.	81
Sebastani, P.	26
Segalowicz, S.	30
Self-Acceptance	60, 61
Self-Esteem	60
Seligman, M.	7
Selye, H.	6, 90
Senescence	18
Sher, J.	15
Silicon	85
Sombrutski, B.	45
Somerfield, L.	15
Statistics Canada	19
Strength Training	3
Stress	6, 37
Stressor	13
Struss, D.	44
Successful Aging	55, 56, 58
Superoxide	27, 28, 29
Supplements	216-217

INDEX

T
TA-65	81
Tai Chi	73
Telomerase	28, 29, 58, 72, 81
Telomere	4, 28, 29, 35, 58, 72
Testosterone	102-104
Thalamus	15, 46
Thompson, P.	9
Tibilone	102
Tierney, M.	50
Time Capsule	31

U
US National Academy Of Sciences	26

V
Vaillant, G.	57, 68, 105
Valliant, P.	72, 74, 79, 93, 130, 131, 133
VanderWerf, Y.	46
Vegetables	198-202
Verbal Information	42
reasoning	30
Viagara	106
Vilcabamba	25
Vitamins	82, 213-216

W
Wallace	105
Wechsler	31
Welsh, M.	15

Werner, C.	72
White Blood Cells	37
Willauer, E.	127
Wine	86
Wong, P.	157

Y

Yalom, I.	69
Yin, Yang	22, 92
Yoga	73

CPSIA information can be obtained at www.ICGtesting.com
Printed in the USA
LVOW070555291212

313676LV00002B/2/P